The World Was Flooded with Light

The World Was Flooded with Light

A Mystical Experience Remembered

Genevieve W. Foster

Commentary by David J. Hufford

University of Pittsburgh Press

Published by the University of Pittsburgh Press, Pittsburgh, Pa., 15260
Copyright © 1985, University of Pittsburgh Press
All rights reserved
Feffer and Simons, Inc., London
Manufactured in the United States of America

Library of Congress Cataloging in Publication Data

Foster, Genevieve W.
  The world was flooded with light.

  Bibliography: p. 187.
  Includes index.
  1. Mysticism.   2. Visions.   3. Foster, Genevieve W.
I. Hufford, David.   II. Title.
BL625.F66   1985   291.4′2   84-22013
ISBN 0-8229-3512-0

Contents

Acknowledgments

In struggling to formulate this very difficult material over a period of years I have been greatly dependent on the encouragement and advice of family and friends. Members of my immediate family have been involved throughout this period, furnishing support, advice, criticism, and much practical help. Especially involved have been my husband, Roger Foster, and my children Charles and Barbara Wakeman, Roger Jr. and Joan Foster, and Jane Foster Buckwalter. My grandsons James and Stephen Wakeman read and responded to an early version of the essay both verbally and in writing, and another grandson, Charles Foster, carefully proofread the essay for me after its final typing. Among my friends and extended family, Nancy Carbonara generously gave me a detailed critique of the first draft, and Ella Calhoun and the late Robert Calhoun gave advice throughout the writing, including a careful review of my final version which Bob Calhoun wrote in the last weeks of his life. Others who read the manuscript at various times and responded with encouragement and criticism and in some cases with very practical help are Marion Bartlett Freeman, Ross Hainline, Dorsha Hayes, Eleanore Kroner, Margaret McFarland, Marion Morris, Alma Paulsen-Hoyer, and Karen VanderVen. I am most grateful to them all; without their support I should not have had the courage to publish. If I have omitted anyone from the list, I hope it may be laid not to ingratitude but to the absent-mindedness of old age. Some others have read this essay and have responded either with enthusiasm or with a reaction that may be summed up as "Thank you, but I don't know what you're talking about." A few have shared with me accounts of crucial events in their own lives. A number of friends and family members have allowed me to quote from letters or other unpublished documents in illustration of various points. I am especially indebted to Doris Albrecht, Librarian of the Kristine Mann Library of the Analytical Psychology Club of New York, who has been helpful beyond the call of duty, and to Joseph E. Jeffs, Librarian of the Georgetown University Library, who kindly put the resources of that library at my disposal. My thanks go to Toni Bouchard, who typed the manuscript and patiently made numerous revisions in the text. And very special gratitude goes to my collaborator David Hufford, who has furnished an objective background for my highly subjective essay, and to Frederick A. Hetzel, Director,

Acknowledgments

and Catherine Marshall, Managing Editor, of the
University of Pittsburgh Press, for their real understanding and their editorial help.

GWF

I am indebted to the editorial staff of the University of Pittsburgh Press for having invited me to
join Genevieve Foster in working on this project,
and to Gen for having been willing to share so
generously with me. Robert Sevensky, my colleague, was always willing to read drafts of the
manuscript; his reassurance and advice, coming
from one trained in religious studies, was very
helpful to me. And I must also thank Marshall
Jones, my chairman in our Department of Behavioral Science of the Pennsylvania State University
College of Medicine, for his assistance and encouragement in my development of the Medical Eth-
nography Collection of the George T. Harrell
Library, the research collection from which most
of my comparative materials are drawn.

DJH

Foreword

David J. Hufford

This book is composed of two interconnected essays. The first is Genevieve Foster's account of a mystical vision that came unexpected and uninvited into the midst of her life. In it she describes the place of that experience in her life, and the peculiar situation in which modern culture places one who has a visionary experience without the benefit of a visionary tradition. This account will be of interest to a variety of audiences. Because of Gen's background in Jungian psychology and her involvement in the very beginnings of analytic psychology in the United States, and because she provides a detailed picture of the connections that she sees between her vision and her Jungian outlook, her narrative will be fascinating for those interested in depth psychology. Because she gives an intimate description of the effects she feels her vision has had on her life for almost forty years, it is a unique document for students of mystical experiences. Perhaps most important, though, is the fact that by deciding to break our culture's rules about who should admit to such experiences she offers some much needed company to others who have been isolated by those rules. For there is a rather spectacular fact that is only dimly recognized in the West: experiences precisely like the one that Gen encountered, plus a number of distinct but related experiences, are as common today as they ever were, and that is very common indeed.

My own essay comprises an introduction to the present state of knowledge about mystical experience generally, and a discussion of Gen's experience in particular. For purposes of comparison, both are illustrated by examples of the mystical experiences of others. This essay has grown out of the opportunity to meet Gen, to talk with her about her experience and subsequent life, and to discuss my efforts to understand the meaning and significance of her experience. I believe that scholarship always benefits by making itself accessible to those under scholarly discussion. In that respect, it has been a privilege to work with Gen on this project and to have her help in bringing into harmony the perspectives of insider and outsider on this most intimate and personal of all subjects.

Perhaps our primary audience, then, will be those individuals who, like Gen, have had an experience the reality and importance of which they cannot deny, yet who live in a society that insists that such experiences can be neither real nor important (except, perhaps, as symptoms of a disordered mind). For those individuals the central burden of this book must be to provide some of the context and guidance that in most other cultures and times would have come more readily to hand.

The World Was Flooded with Light

These ideas are only fantasies. When you have abandoned any and all creeds, all you have left are fantasies to tell you the nature of the unseen world. But I have learned over a long lifetime to take my fantasies seriously. *As for the experience of intellectual vision that I had in mid-life, that was not fantasy, that was an experience of Reality, so that I can say with Jung, I do not believe, I know.*

Reminiscence

This essay started as a simple account of certain experiences, certain manifestations of the unconscious, which occurred many years ago and which have seemed to me sufficiently interesting, sufficiently remarkable at least in their occurring to one of my highly rational upbringing and education, so that I did not want to go out of the world without leaving some account of them. These events took place at the conclusion of a Jungian analysis that had gone on, with various interruptions, for some twelve years. The account of them that I wrote many years later was intended for my immediate family only. A Jungian analyst who saw a portion of this account, but who was otherwise a stranger to me, suggested that if it could be published along with some commentary; either before or after my death, it would be "a contribution to depth psychology." He naturally had in mind a

Jungian audience; I, however, had misgivings. Although I consider myself a Jungian, I have lived and worked outside the Jungian circle, among Freudians and others, and I have learned to modify my language so as to communicate with them after a fashion. Moreover, the Jungians have developed over the years an extensive language of symbolism with which I am not entirely familiar. I doubt if the essay I have to write would fit in with what I see published in the Jungian journals (and this observation does not in the least question the value of what is published there).

I am sure that there will be a relative rapprochement of the analytical schools in the years to come, and I hope my essay will find its place somewhere in the area where the schools begin to overlap. But since I have to write while I am still extant, I will address myself to whom it may concern, and the future will have to take care of itself. My essay is made up of three parts. The first is a bit of history. In trying to give some context to the experiences I have mentioned, I had to speculate first how they came about, what led up to them, and this led me to a review of my analysis and of my relation to the other members of the Analytical Psychology Club in the nineteen thirties and early forties. Although it is a very personal, certainly not unbiased account, it may be of interest as a sort of limited view of the early days of Jungian analysis in this country. This leads directly to the account of the manifestation of the unconscious that is the core of the essay. The third part is a description of the sort of informal theorizing that has been going on in my head over the past thirty-five years—my attempt to make sense of my own life, of other people's lives, in the light of that very important experience. Why did the unconscious speak so decisively to me at what would now be called the midpoint of life? (We had no such term then.) Does this happen to others? I have been much influenced by the work that has been done in describing and illuminating the sequence of human development by Erikson, by the English psychoanalytic observers, and others. But I find that my Jungian bias, and especially my awareness of the way in which the collective unconscious intervenes at the crisis points of human development—hands up, as it were, archetypal fantasies that become patterns for the life course—all this has provided me with a somewhat different way of looking at the sequence of human development, has given me a set of intuitive half-formulated ideas which have put themselves together underground, I might say, while I was doing other, more urgent, more practical things. At this late date, I cannot give body and conviction to these thoughts; I can only adumbrate them. But I think that they are important, and I hope that other, younger people will pick them up and work with them either because they are stimulated by what I have to say or because they come upon them independently.

My analytic notes no longer exist, and it is impossible to recall the series of dreams and fantasies that led up to what was a decisive encounter with the Other. But though I am, in the words of my analyst, "an introvert from Introvertsville," much of the struggle that preceded this encounter occurred in the outer world, in my interaction with my analyst, whose view of events diverged increasingly from mine, and with the other Jungian analysands of those early days. Of a part of this interaction I have vivid memories, and some of it I can document. It seems to me that an account of this human interchange would be the best setting I could offer to the later, subjective experiences, because it is concerned with a phase of analysis that I think has not been much written about, the phase when the analysand struggles to assimilate the final and most important projections which form part of an intense transference. If part of the story I am about to tell sounds like what might have gone on in a girls' school with several headmistresses in charge—well, that is how I remember it.

I am now eighty-two years old. I became enthusiastic about Jung when I was twenty-two, when a theologian friend, later to become my brother-in-law, lent me a copy of Jung's *Psychology of the Unconscious.* I started analysis when I was thirty with Dr. Esther Harding, one of the pioneers of Jungian analysis in this country. Analysis is a struggle toward greater consciousness, often painful when one encounters the various aspects of one's own "shadow side," but nevertheless deeply rewarding. Dr. Harding was an excellent analyst, a gifted woman with a beautiful quality of intuition and an ability to use a strong positive transference creatively, and I owe her much. There were interruptions for various reasons, but nevertheless there seemed to be much progress. In the account of the struggle which ensued, I would not want to minimize the transformation that took place, nor the vistas of meaning and of feeling that were opened up for me. This story starts at the point when, after several fruitful years, our respective understandings of my inner state began to diverge in an increasingly serious way.

Let me pause to say that in the years of which I am writing, I was the wife of a busy attorney and the mother of a growing family, and I very often had, in addition, a part or full-time teaching job. Analysis was, therefore, not the whole of my life. But, in the time that I could devote to it, it was very important. To get back to my difference with Dr. Harding, it seemed to me that certain of my analytic material which had a creative denotation, or a creative content, was being consistently disparaged, shunted aside, and so far as I permitted this interpretation, tended to disappear from my awareness, not to be important any longer. To the extent that we differed, she and I were talking about two different people. To the extent that I concurred in what I basically knew was a false interpretation, my own personality was narrowed, and we were analysing a hypothetical person, not the real person that I was. I tried in innumerable ways to point out this dilemma to her; but to her the situation seemed quite different. To her it seemed as though what appeared to me as creativity was an "animus delusion," and only by sacrificing this conviction of creativity could I progress in

my analysis. This I believe is not an unusual situation in analysis, and the interpretation Dr. Harding was giving me is a usual one, and I assume it
is usually right. In my case it was not. I understood very well what she was trying to do. She
was trying to help me subdue my ego to the point
where a greater and more important value could
emerge. But this was not, for me, the way to do it,
and I was resisting. Words are ambiguous in these
situations, and again and again I thought we had
come to an agreement—that there were two kinds
of creativity, one more ego-bound than the other—
only to find her again responding reductively to
material which I felt had a constructive meaning.
We didn't quarrel; we both tried earnestly and for
a long time to come to some understanding, but
in vain. Finally, in the spring of 1937, I reluc-
tantly told her I was discontinuing my work with
her. She seemed very surprised. She had apparently
thought of me as a deeply committed analysand,
as indeed I was. "You of all people," she said. I
tried to explain that I was, I hoped, not abandoning
my inner development; I was not even necessarily
abandoning my analysis; I was simply stopping
work with her. But we had reached such a pitch of
misunderstanding that there seemed to be no fine
distinctions. I felt that I was out of the fold.

If Dr. Harding had been as wise as I wanted
her to be, I might have continued to be her devoted disciple, and the struggle for separation that
then ensued might not have taken place, or it
might have come later, and in a different form. As
it was, though we remained friendly, there was a

permanent misunderstanding. It was not easy to make the break, and I made it with great anxiety. It was impossible to rupture my intense transference suddenly, essential as it seemed to do so. The fall of that year was the occasion of Dr. Jung's second American seminar, this one to be given in New York. I had heard that when he had been in New York the previous year, some people had had individual appointments with him, and I wrote to him in Zurich to ask if he could possibly see me. He responded that he could. "Please tell Dr. Bertine that she puts you on my list." (Dr. Bertine was a colleague of Dr. Harding's, another one of the Jungian analysts.)

I was allotted half an hour with Dr. Jung. It seemed impossible to lay so complex a problem before him, and to get appropriate advice, within so short a time. But I rehearsed what I had to say until I had reduced it to the most concise form possible and marshaled a certain amount of unconscious material that I thought relevant, and went to my appointment. Dr. Jung was holding his consultations in the sitting room of a New York hotel suite. He was a big man, well over six feet, and solidly built. I can still remember the intensity of his gaze which he directed at me through his thin-rimmed glasses as he leaned forward in his seat. Even before I came to the end of my recital he began to nod vigorously. "You must do what you have decided," he said, "because that is your own individual way" (he pronounced it *individwal*) "and you must follow it even at the risk of your life." This was so subversive in the

light of what Dr. Harding had been saying that I
began to raise the question whether she might possibly be right. "Dr. Harding iss only a woman," he
said. "She doesn't know everything." And then he
grinned. He had what I can only describe as a
square grin; the corners of his mouth turned up
more or less at right angles, and the effect on this
occasion was a bit diabolical. We were perhaps ten
minutes into the half hour and I had presented my
business and had my answer, but I wasn't about to
say thank you and go away; I was determined to
have the other twenty minutes. I had expected
him to ask a great many questions. He had asked
none. I said lamely, in defense of Dr. Harding,
that I thought perhaps I needed someone to talk
to. "Whom do you think I talk to?" he demanded. "I
talk to people like yourself, and when they don't
understand me, then I make them. Dr. Harding
will never understand you," he went on. "Find
your milieu. Find the people who will understand
you. Talk to them." Some of the few people to
whom I have told this story have expressed amaze-
ment that Dr. Jung would make so firm a pro-
nouncement on so short an acquaintance. To this
I can only respond that although he did not know
me, he knew Dr. Harding very well; and further
that the unconscious material I had given him,
dreams and the like, from the time when I made
the break from her, was pretty cogent. Anyway,
this was no ordinary man; this man was a tower-
ing genius. His last advice had been so far from
my comprehension that I abandoned that line of
discussion. But since there was still time left I

asked a question about the group mandala which he had seen and about which he had commented the evening before. But that entails a whole story which I shall first have to tell.

Because we were living near New York during the year 1936–1937 I had the pleasure of participating in the monthly meetings of the Education Group of the Analytical Psychology Club. The club was the New York Jungian organization and was only a few years old. Those of us who were members were becoming acquainted with one another and were exploring, some of us at least, the experience of an intense group relationship. I did not actually live in New York during these years, and some of the time I was not within easy commuting distance. Since most of my energy was absorbed by family and job outside the Jungian group, I was always a relative outsider. But this year I was living close enough to participate in many activities of the club, and I made the most of it. It was, I think, the first year of the Education Group, comprising some ten or twelve people, most of whom were teachers. Most of us were analysands of one or another of the three doctors whom we came to call collectively "the Analysts," Drs. Eleanor Bertine, Esther Harding, and Kristine Mann. But there was also in the Education Group Dr. Bruno Klopfer, a psychologist refugee from Nazism who was to become well known for introducing the Rorschach Test into the United States. He had worked with Dr. Jung, and I was under the impression at the time that he had been accepted as a referring analyst to the club, which would

have meant that his analysands, after a certain
number of hours and upon his recommendation,
could become club members. Dr. Alma Paulsen,
who was also there, tells me I was probably mistaken in this matter, and she is probably right.
There seem to be no existing records. There was
also a lay analyst whom I shall call Miss J. She
had been analyzed in Zurich and was thus eligible
for club membership, but she had definitely not
been accepted as a referring analyst to the club,
which meant that her patients could not become
members. The regulations for club membership
have not, I think, changed over the years. But in
those early years, there was no analytic institute
for training Jungian analysts, not even in Zurich.
Nor was there any professional association of
Jungian analysts. The early New York analysts
had been analyzed by Jung and had then started
practice in this country with his encouragement.
At the time of which I am writing, a place on the
roster of referring analysts, with the privilege of
recommending patients as club members, was tan-
tamount to accreditation as a Jungian analyst; at
least it was the nearest thing to accreditation that
there was. But the bylaws of the club were enacted not by the analysts alone but by the entire
membership. This was probably the best arrange-
ment that could have been made at the time. A
professional organization of three or four medical
analysts would scarcely have been viable. If an organization had been formed of all the self-appointed
analysts, it would have been impossible to uphold

any reasonable standards for training or practice. This actually happened elsewhere, where there were no Jungian medical analysts or clinical psychologists to protest, and with lamentable results. But we, as club members, were thus in the uneasy position of deciding collectively what the process should be by which a Jungian analyst could be recognized as such in New York City. In a faithful version of the democratic process, we had entrusted the power of decision to our representatives, the Medical Board of the club; in practice, we mostly voted the opinions of our respective analysts. Since most of the people in the Club were patients of the Analysts, that is, the three established medical analysts, they could always count on a majority. This is a long digression, but it helps to explain the group process of which we now found ourselves a part. Most of us in the Education Group were working with one of the Analysts, but there were people in the group who were themselves analysts; they were, however, not *our* analysts.

We began that year by reading short papers to one another about our work with, or observations of, children. Miss J. and I read papers on the same evening. Hers was an attempt, and as I look back on it a brave and good one, to explore the dynamics between herself and a young niece. If I remember correctly, the child used to wet her bed only when Miss J. was in charge of her, and Miss J. had been able to explore the unconscious strands in the relationship in such a way that the bedwetting stopped. I do not remember any criticism during the discussion, although I became (silently) offended at Miss J. when I thought she suggested that my paper was superficial in relation to hers. But her paper must not have been entirely well received, or perhaps there was an earlier paper which I had missed; some time later one of the group members referred (not in her presence) to something she had written as a "strip-tease." At any rate, she was perhaps not entirely comfortable in the group, for if I remember correctly (and I am writing more than forty years after the event) she very soon dropped out and did not return. Soon thereafter, at another of the monthly meetings, there was a heated discussion in which most of the group disagreed with Dr. Klopfer; he found himself maintaining a position that was under ideological attack from most of the group membership. I cannot remember what the argument was about, nor whether I disagreed with him or agreed or was neutral, but I know that although I liked him personally and formed a friendship with him that outlasted our membership in the Education Group, I sometimes found his psychological opinions unacceptable, too "Freudian"—they did not represent the way in which I had read Jung, or the way in which my analyst had interpreted Jung to me. At any rate, there was a heated argument of which he was the focus, and for whatever reason, while I am not sure that he dropped out of the group permanently, he was absent from most of the meetings that winter and thus was not with us for the adventure of the group mandala.[1] Perhaps, it occurs to me, he simply found that business too silly, and stayed away until it was over. At any rate, all those now left in the group were patients of the Analysts, except perhaps for one or two analysands of Mrs. Frances Wickes, a pupil of Jung's who had been in practice as long as they had. Somehow or other, the two outside authorities had been extruded from the group, and we insiders had now only one another as targets for any negative feelings that might come up.

I have been urged by my Jungian readers not to reveal the identities of any of the people involved in this story except, of course, Dr. Jung. But this is a bit of history, recounted with whatever biases are necessary to me, but still history, and I would like it to be as authentic as possible. There is, however, a certain impropriety in revealing the names of patients in analysis, which I suppose I should observe even though very few of us are still living. Members of the APC necessarily knew each others' names; if you wanted to preserve anonymity you did not join the APC. In the account that follows, I will use first names only, except in the case of analysts; present members of the APC who are old enough to have known these people will probably recognize them, while outsiders almost certainly will not.

---

1. *Mandala* is a Sanskrit word meaning circle. The spontaneous appearance of circular symbolism in dreams and fantasy was the subject of Jung's American seminars in 1936 and 1937. The reader will find this material in the fourth section of his book *The Integration of the Personality.*

I am not sure what it was that deflected us from the discussion of children—the proper concern of an education group—to consideration of ourselves as a group. There was one meeting from which I was absent during which, I was told, Leah reproached Sallie for something she had said, for some opinion or attitude, and feelings were hurt, especially Sallie's. It may be that we expected harmony among us, and never seemed to achieve it. In the mid-thirties, none of the studies of group dynamics that were to be so useful later, was yet available. S. R. Slavson's book, *An Introduction to Group Therapy,* was to come out in 1943. But it began to occur to me, and I believe to others, that our group was an organism of some sort. I remember having an opportunity some time that year to search the card catalogue of the Library of Congress for works on group psychology, and I found none, or none of any consequence. Nor can I remember just how or when the question arose whether a group could draw a collective mandala. It may have arisen during a committee meeting held in a restaurant called The President on Lexington Avenue, comprising Sallie, Estelle, and me, and perhaps one other person. We had one drink each, which in our abstemious lives was enough to make us rather inventive. I do remember that that was the afternoon when for the only time in my life I lost my pocketbook containing money, keys, and driver's license.

At any rate, the proposal that we draw a collective mandala was made to the whole group by one or more of us. There was discussion; some were opposed but the majority were in favor. It took some time, perhaps a month or so, before we fully made up our minds. Why it had to be a mandala, why we couldn't draw just any picture, I can't remember. But meantime word of what we were up to reached the analysts one way and another, and they hastily set about to put a stop to it, speaking to us individually as we came in for our respective hours, describing it as a rash and even dangerous venture, an unwise meddling with the unconscious. Somehow we persisted. One of our group was the sister of one of the analysts. Surely they must have put pressure on her, but she never said anything about it and she persisted along with the rest of us. From correspondence that still exists, I find that I thought at the time that the original suggestion had come either from her or from me. But once the idea was proposed, other people became more enthusiastic than we had been. The person most keen for the venture was Sallie, one of the people involved in forming the Analytical Psychology Club in the first place and one of its most active members. For some reason this experiment was very important to her. She was, I gradually came to realize, uncomfortable in the group in spite of her active participation, not only in the Education Group but in the little group of analysands that formed the active core of the APC. She was not deliberately "picked on"; all the group members were serious analysands and conscious of a real bond; but when there were differences of opinion, it was often Sallie who was felt to be in the wrong. I think perhaps

she hoped for some change, some greater consciousness on all hands, which might come as a
result of this group venture. So it was she that
provided the materials, the big sheet of brown
wrapping paper on which we were to draw, and
the box of chalks. She had already drawn a big
circle on the paper. The paper was placed on a
large table in the middle of the room and we sat
around it and, rather in the manner of a Quaker
meeting, when the spirit moved we stepped forward and drew something in the circle. My memory is that since a circle was already drawn, we
tended to balance whatever we drew; that is, if we
drew a design, we would put in three similar de-
signs at equal intervals around the circle. (We had
heard Dr. Jung lecture extensively on mandalas
last year and this.) For my part, I had no inspiration until most of the other members had made
their contribution, but watched with a certain as-
tonishment as people drew figures in pink, pale
blue, lavender, and (it seemed to me) other anemic
colors. On an impulse, I took up a dark chalk and
drew in four shapes at equal intervals that I would
have described as arrowheads or direction mark-
ers. Dr. Jung later called them "hooks," and this
was appropriate because one fin was longer than
the other. They seemed to suggest a rotary motion, or to add to whatever motion was already in
the picture. I cannot now remember whether the
motion was clockwise or counterclockwise, but I
suspect it was the latter. At some point I think
somebody added something in red. Sallie, who had
been so eager for the group picture, in the end

drew nothing in herself. She wanted, she told me
later, to draw some little ailerons, like those on an
airplane—something, I suppose, that would indicate an ability within the group to control its own
direction—but she was so upset by this time by
the attitude toward her of some of the group members that she could not bring herself to do so. It
was she who afterward kept the picture, and I
have no idea what happened to it ultimately. So
far as any of us could see, the dire consequences
predicted by the analysts never came about. Nobody went off the deep end. Perhaps the groupish-
ness of our group was enhanced by our venture.
Perhaps if we had let well enough alone, the poles
of leadership and scapegoat would not have been
so fully constellated as they were, and Sallie, who
suffered most from this phenomenon, would have
been at least partially spared. Or perhaps the picture
only represented what was already in the group.

It was Sallie who took charge of the group picture and it was she who persuaded Dr. Jung to
meet with us and to comment on it. The meeting
took place, if I remember correctly, half an hour
or so before one of his lectures, in an anteroom of
the auditorium where he was to speak. The picture
was spread on a table, and we all stood around it.
I cannot remember most of his comments, but he
took it seriously. He did not tell us that a group
could not draw such a picture, as Dr. Bertine was
to do in her lecture on the group. From the existing
correspondence I know that he told us that our
picture represented a totalitarian group, that it could
have been drawn in Nazi Germany. What I do re-

member vividly was what he said when he pointed to the figures I had drawn in. "These hooks," he said, "these are of the devil." I felt disgraced before the group and somewhat conscience-stricken.

So when I found there was extra time in my precious half-hour with Dr. Jung the next day, I brought up this problem. I was the one, I told him, who had drawn those devilish hooks and what he said had dismayed me. "But you saw what was missing in the group picture," he said, "and you put it in." I had had a dream the previous night, the night between his commenting on our picture and my appointment with him, and I told it to him now. I thought it referred to my dismay over what he had said about my contribution to the picture, and by inference about my role in the group. A man and a woman were riding in a car. The man was driving; the woman in the seat beside him seemed to be in some way both myself and not myself. A child was riding in the back seat, and suddenly this child fell off the seat. That was the whole dream. Dr. Jung inquired whether the man who was driving was the husband of the woman. Yes, I said, it seemed to me so. "Then it is not the unknown animus," he said.[2] "Then it is

---

2. This is Jung's term for the important archetype (which he also calls the *Soul*) which is normally projected on the important man in a woman's life, father, husband, son, or masculine mentor. The counterpart in a man's psyche is the *anima*. See the chapter on "Animus and Anima" in *Two Essays on Analytical Psychology*, and the entries under "Soul" and "Soul Image" in *Psychological Types*. The implication of his remarks here is that the woman in the dream is not being carried off by a stranger, she is driving with someone she loves and trusts, i.e., what she is doing is legitimate.

perfectly all right. Chust pick the child up and put it back on the seat." He offered no other interpretation and I asked for none. We were talking in intuitive shorthand. But I did say that I seemed to have made trouble in the group and I was sorry about it. "Oh," he said cheerfully, "there will be trouble wherever you go." I must have looked crestfallen at this because he grinned again. "Oh, that is not so bad," he said. "Look at me. There is trouble wherever I go. First there are great enthusiasms and then there are great resistances and then there is trouble. Some people think I am the devil incarnate." He went on to talk further about the dynamics of the creative person vis-à-vis the group, drawing much on his own experience. I am rather embarrassed to recount all this, having made so small a contribution after all the fuss, but I can see that he simply took me at my word and gave me the full treatment. Whether I could use his advice or not was my problem.

I do not want to leave the story of the group mandala without saying a little more about Sallie. She had an interview with Dr. Jung, too, and she told me a little about it. She is dead now, and I hope her loving shade will forgive me—for it cannot be other than loving—if I repeat what she told me, for greater enlightenment and because it is pertinent to the discussion here. "They don't understand you," Jung said to her. She was an analysand of Dr. Bertine's but had done some work with Dr. Harding when Dr. Bertine was abroad. "They don't understand you. You are all over splinters and wherever they touch you, it hurts. When

I touch you, it doesn't hurt. You do what you can.
You bring your material to analysis, and they
don't understand you." Sallie cried, and he reached
over and took her hand and held it. So far as she
told me, he gave her no advice; but several years
later she left analysis, left New York, and found a
different job in another state. I think her communications with her New York friends gradually diminished. Certainly, after a few years, my not
very frequent letters went unanswered. Perhaps
she needed to forget all of us.

The events in the Education Group that I have
described, together with what I had heard and
seen of the wider interaction of the Jungian analysands living in New York, had influenced me profoundly, and I had thought about it all a great
deal. I had begun to see that a group, at least a
group in which there is so much emotional interchange, tends to generate a leader or leaders on
the one hand and one or more scapegoats on the
other. I am sure this was not an original idea with
me; it was one of those things in the air at the
time. But I had seen it happening rather dramati-
cally. In the same year in which the adventure of
the group mandala took place, and in the previous
year, I had watched and participated in a very different kind of group interaction in another setting,
namely the effort of a small minority to radicalize
a teachers' union. I was too naive, as were many
of my colleagues, to recognize at first what the
real issues were. Those were the days before Communist party tactics were widely understood, and
none of the people involved admitted at the time

to being a Communist. I could only see that something very strange was going on, a determined effort to use democratic procedures to undermine
the democratic process itself. This effort the rest
of us countered by conscientiously attending all
the meetings and voting our principles, and all
their efforts failed; but the efforts were persistent
and repeated, and we had to be on the alert constantly. The contrast between this piece of group
interaction and the interaction I had seen and
taken part of in the APC was instructive. It
seemed to me (when I finally began to understand
what was going on) that in the union the small
group, the radicals, had projected the authority archetype to a leadership outside our group—they
had given up their own consciences, in fact—and
were doing the bidding of that leadership while
the rest of us, fortunately a majority, were listening to the authority within ourselves. For although in this case we were, it is true, doing what
the college administration very much wanted
done, we were doing it not because they wanted it
but because we thought it right. We had on other
occasions opposed the wishes of the administration and usually had made our opposition stick.

The analytic group, on the other hand, was
made up by the very nature of the analytic process
of people many of whom had projected authority
and much else to their analysts, giving the analysts a temporary but extraordinary influence. Besides this, we had at that time over the water the
awful example of Nazi Germany, where almost
the entire nation, in a sort of mass lunacy, had

projected authority and everything else that was good to the Führer, while the Jews and sometimes Gentiles who were sane enough to keep their heads were singled out and persecuted. Most of us were aware that terrible things were going on in Germany, although at that date, 1937, the worst was yet to come.

During the next year, my geographic distance from New York and the birth of my youngest child kept me from taking any active part in club affairs, but a few papers that I have preserved show that I was maintaining a lively interest in the club. Among these papers I find a carbon copy of Dr. Bertine's lecture on "The Individual and the Group," with the words "Not proofread" scrawled on the first page in Sallie's handwriting. Sallie must have been the typist for Dr. Bertine, and must have put in an extra carbon for me. The paper was given to the club in October 1939. The statement that Dr. Bertine makes that a group is not an individual and thus cannot draw a mandala refers of course to our venture of two years before. Dr. Bertine and Dr. Harding (and perhaps also Dr. Mann, whom I knew only by sight) had a fear of groups that is hard today to explain; they seemed to think of a group as something that could degenerate easily into a mob, mindless and out of control. They were firmly opposed to group psychotherapy. Younger colleagues finally forced that issue, years later. I well remember the evening when Dr. Whitmont gave a paper on group psychotherapy and Dr. Edinger, in the ensuing discussion, supported him saying, "We can't go on forever running away from this," or words to that effect. But in 1939 and 1940 these younger colleagues were not in the picture, and those of us who wanted to understand the group in a less negative way were getting no encouragement whatever from the leadership.

Among the papers that I still have is the carbon copy of a long letter from me to Alma Paulsen (not yet Dr. Paulsen and not yet an analyst), who I think must then have been chairman of the Education Group. Written in the spring of 1939, it was an effort to understand something of the structure of our group, starting with Dr. Jung's statement that our picture was that of a totalitarian group. I suggested that Alma share my letter with the Education Group if they were still interested in the subject, and I apparently thought it important enough so that I circulated copies of it further, at least to Ellen and Hildegard, and finally to Dr. Bertine, with whom I had some correspondence following her paper on the group and later following the one-act play which she wrote and read at a club meeting in 1940, the subject of which was a small group of people in a country about to be taken over by a totalitarian dictatorship. I still have carbons of my two long letters to her and her two long, handwritten, carefully reasoned replies.

Beyond all this I was distressed for Sallie — distressed because of the role she had occupied and still seemed to occupy in the group. Dr. Jung's "They don't understand you," still rang in my ears. It is easy to look at the situation now and to say that the leadership should have observed what the group tended to project to her and what it was that she did to invite these projections, but this is hindsight. People didn't think in those terms in those days. I am sure they tried to help her, or specifically Dr. Bertine did, and I am sure the situation was seen entirely as Sallie's problem. What I began to see, or thought I did, was that she really *was* misunderstood, she served as scapegoat for the leadership just as she did for the rest. In other words, in this area of understanding, our leaders were just as unconscious as we were. They had even mistaken her type, or so it seemed to me.[3] She passed for a thinking introvert; that was her analyst's opinion. But it seemed to me that her thinking processes were laborious, not especially under the control of her ego, but that her feeling, while shy and not ostentatious, was always ready. It was she to whom her family turned to break the news to their mother that the mother's beloved sister had just died. And I remember her holding my small daughter, saying over and over, "She is the *sweetest* baby," and making the baby laugh for the first time ever as she coaxed the puppy to play on the sofa beside them. And, some years later, I remember her sitting down and crying when the box came containing the civilian clothes of her much-loved and orphaned nephew, now drafted and

---

3. This refers to Jung's classification of psychological types. A description of the eight types (which become sixteen if one considers the secondary function) can be found toward the end of his *Psychological Types.* It is interesting to me that he says that the introverted feeling type is often not recognized.

in uniform. And giving warm hospitality to my own son, in his seaman's uniform and away from home. What do you do if your analyst mistakes your type and sees you upside down?

Right or wrong, I was wrestling with these ideas when I undertook to write a paper for the *Bulletin* of the APC on the nature of the group— our group. I was feeling more and more strongly that we in the analytic group, since greater individual consciousness was our aim, ought to be more conscious also of the nature of our group participation. And implied in this effort was the idea that our leaders, our analysts, were as unconscious in this area as we were—that all of us together had to struggle for awareness. Additionally, I must have had all sorts of unconscious motivations. I was, you might say, in the midst of my analytic adolescence. The paper, which cost me a good deal of thought and time to write, was submitted to the *Bulletin* committee and was returned to me twice for clarification of key ideas. In order not to shock my audience too much I had suggested or adumbrated a part of what I had to say, leaving an astute reader to draw conclusions and hoping not to hurt too many feelings. I was afraid specifically that what I said might be construed as an attack on the analysts. But Ellen or Hildegard or both were on the *Bulletin* committee that year, and they and perhaps others were given to rigorous thinking processes. It is possible that they thought that in those places where I had softpedaled my observations I was not sure of what I myself meant. For whatever reason, they insisted on having all ideas spelled out in full, so that the final revision produced a pretty forthright document. The paper, which was finally published in the December 1940 *Bulletin*, attempted to formulate the idea that because of the prevalent transferences of patients to analysts, ours was by nature and necessity a sort of totalitarian group. If we could become more aware of the way in which we as a group functioned, we could, I thought, make a real contribution to the understanding of group behavior.

I was afraid that my observations would seem to drop on the membership like a ton of bricks, and I was really apprehensive about the reaction of my fellow club members. Although I was in New York on the date of the next club meeting, I was almost afraid to go. But I did go, in fear and trembling, and to the everlasting credit of my friends and acquaintances in the club, they all greeted me kindly, even those who were to attack my article vigorously in the next issue of the *Bulletin*. Only Leah reproached me, some time later. I should have realized, she said, not only that such an article would dominate this issue of the *Bulletin*, but that the next couple of issues would be taken up with discussion about it, leaving no space for articles on other more important subjects. It has since occurred to me that my relative immunity from attack arose from the fact that the real rivalries within the group were going on among Dr. Bertine's patients. She seems to me to have been the popular analyst of that period, and the conspicuous interaction was among the Bertinites, of which I was not one. And then there was a general wish on all sides to understand and to reason, rather than to condemn. For my paper had indeed shocked the club considerably. Four members wrote indignant rebuttals in the next issue, while a fifth article, by Hildegard, maintained a more judicial tone.

One of the papers, by Marie, in particular I thought required an answer. She had drawn a contrast between the unfortunate individual who must give his allegiance to the "deified state" and the individual (presumably like us here in the club) who has the "redemptive hope of a counter process" whereby the "mark of divinity" might "be taken back from the projection and set again, by each individual, upon his own brow." This formulation drove me to an answer, in which I tried to point out that the use of the word *individual* was for all of us ambiguous. We used *individual* as meaning one pole of a pair of opposites, the other being the group. On the other hand, we used the term *individuality* as meaning the reconciling principle between pairs of opposites, including the group-individual pair. I protested vigorously against the idea of "setting the mark of divinity" on one's own brow. One must at all costs avoid identifying oneself with the central value; that way lies lunacy. This paper came out in the February 1941 issue of the *Bulletin* along with one signed B. K. (Bruno Klopfer) implicitly supporting my position, and undertaking to clarify what my critics *thought* I was saying. The paper I wrote on this occasion caused me some uneasiness because it seemed to me to draw a distinction that Dr. Jung himself had never made. Therefore I sent him a copy of it. He responded with a little note, "I make no objection to this." This paper, if not the first, began to make sense to the analysts; at least Dr. Bertine told me on some occasion when we met casually that she had liked it. There had been no reaction expressed (to me) about the first paper either from her or from Dr. Harding. I have written this account as though the struggle within me was played out largely in intellectual terms, but actually there was much emotion. The negative feelings toward Dr. Harding, which are as much a part of an intense transference as the positive, asserted themselves through these years. They never totally overwhelmed the positive feelings and the clash between the two was very conscious, but there were times when I could not mention her name without an edge to my voice. Theoretically the analyst's understanding of this struggle should serve to see the patient through, but I had, I think, got into a territory where she could no longer observe me impartially. Some of the things I said to her I think really hurt, and I recall one particularly slanderous dream (which I told her—such are the rules of the game), which seemed really to upset her.

I have described this experience at length because I am convinced that the struggle to convey a message to my Jungian peers (and to the analysts), like the struggle for understanding with my own analyst, was the outward sign of an inner process which led to a profound change. Just how the outer struggle was related to the inner change I am not entirely sure and perhaps wiser heads can throw some light on the matter. This much I can say about such a process. Having failed to gain the understanding of my analyst I had to "go public" in search of understanding; it was, in miniature form, the process the artist or writer goes through who must bring the message from the unconscious to the world, in the hope that somebody "out there" will hear. I think I should repeat here what I said above; analysis was only part of my life. I was very busy with my family and my teaching, and though I no longer have the record of my dreams and fantasies, I was at the same time working continuously, as well as I could manage, with or without help, on my inner development.

Jungian analysands are expected (or were in my day) to keep a record of all their dreams and to write up after every analytic hour as complete an account as they can of what was said during the hour, and in addition they are encouraged to draw, or paint, or write, or use any art form that comes easily to their hand, whether or not what they create is particularly acceptable as art; the products of these more or less artistic efforts are used in the same way as dreams are to study the motions of the unconscious. In November 1941, I wrote the first of four sonnets which became very important to me. They served as a central formulation, valid for life, which I cherished, showed to very few people, and carried around with me folded into my wallet like a talisman. Our home was blessed in those days by a devoted housekeeper who loved the children and was loved by them, and since my husband was supportive of my Jungian activities, although he did not share them, her presence made it possible for me occasionally to get away for a night or so in New York, for an analytic hour or two, for a visit to my Jungian friends, or just to be alone. Each of my sonnets was I believe written in a little room in the East 40th (or maybe it was 39th) Street Allerton House, an inexpensive hostelry for women which was the closest I could come to the room of one's own that Virginia Woolf declares is essential for such undertakings.

One more thing is important. In my early adulthood, as a budding young English teacher, I had put in several years in graduate school, and had embarked on the long road toward the doctorate in English, had finished the necessary courses, passed the formidable general examinations, demonstrated my ability to sight-read in French, German, and Latin, and had undertaken a dissertation on the influence of the Latin hymn on the Middle English religious lyric. I had had several extensions of time and, at the period of which I am writing, the dissertation was still unfinished. Meantime, what with marriage, child-rearing, and analysis, all the interest and excitement had gone out of it, and indeed the pursuit of literary origins had come to seem an impossibly meaningless task. But since I had come up against a deadline, I cobbled together a volume of sorts and submitted it. It was rejected. I had flunked out. Although I knew quite well that what I had submitted was inadequate, I was a good deal chagrined. It was a blow to my pride. It was perhaps the coup de grace to my ego-orientation that Dr. Harding had tried in vain to bring about. But it freed me from further obligation in that field of study. If it had been accepted, I should have been obliged, by my agreement with the university, to publish my findings. Now I was free to venture, as I had long wanted to do, into a field more in line with my analytic interests, which proved in the end to be clinical work with emotionally disturbed children. But in my work on the dissertation I (reared as a Protestant) had had to study the Mass and the Canonical Office and had become acquainted with many of the great hymns of the church and with that body of English verse that expressed the Christian faith of the fourteenth, fifteenth, and sixteenth centuries. Among clergy and laity alike there was in that period a surge of mystical yearning and of mystical experience. For me, especially since I was a Protestant, it was all very far away and long ago and not to be taken seriously except as an object of literary study. But all of it, the tremendous cadences of the Mass, the symbolism of the great hymns, and the simpler English verses, some of which are invocations of mystical experience, must have taken a grip on my unconscious in ways that I was not aware of.

I had not been able, as Dr. Jung advised, to make a clean break with Dr. Harding. With her concurrence, I went for several years for occasional hours with Dr. Margaret Nordfeldt, whom I had met and liked at the time of Dr. Jung's seminar at Bailey Island, Maine, in the fall of 1936.

She was a great help to me. For though she appeared to understand what was going on in me no better than Dr. Harding had, she had a certain faith in the creative process and she was able to stand by and let things happen. She had been an artist's wife and dealt in her work with many artists, writers, and theatrical people, and although I was none of these, her attitude may have been different for that reason. She perhaps lacked something of Dr. Harding's incisiveness, but that no longer mattered so much. Our association led to a friendship that lasted until her death more than thirty years later. But in the end I had to go back to Dr. Harding to retrieve (though I could not have put it in this way at the time) those intense projections, positive and negative, which I had made to her and which I had somehow to get back. These contacts were not frequent, but they occurred once in a while into the year 1945. But we got on no better than before. We still disagreed on the nature of much important material. She was sure that the direction in which I was headed, analytically speaking, was an entirely wrong one, that I was a victim of the misleading animus. No doubt my activities in the Education Group and my communications to the *Bulletin* influenced her view of me. I was still in touch with her when I wrote the last three sonnets of my four (they came in the years 1942 and 1943) and I can still remember some of her comments. She was a medical doctor and had never been taught the art of reading verse; she tended to ignore grammar and syntax and thus sometimes to miss the sense.

She could and did, however, pick out the symbols
in my sonnets which she agreed were of great importance. She knew that they represented the central value. But though she recognized the symbolism, she failed to grasp its purport. What the other
issues between us were at that period I have forgotten, and I no longer have my notes, but we
were as much at odds as ever. Finally, in the
spring of 1945, I told her for the second time that
I was discontinuing my work with her, expressing
at the same time my very genuine gratitude for
the help she had given me earlier. This help had
been material. I was one of those touched early by
death, by the death of a sister when I was very
young, by the death of my first husband, a brilliant young physician, after only three years of
marriage. Without analytic intervention I might
never have found the courage to pick up my life
and marry again. Furthermore, I am convinced,
whatever struggles and mistakes occurred in the
course of my analysis, that without the heightened consciousness it afforded, the experience I
am about to describe could never have occurred.
But the time for parting with her had come. I
think it was at this time that she threatened me
with the prognosis of a breakdown if I stopped my
analytic work. She was very intuitive, and it is
likely she sensed my unusual closeness to the unconscious at this time, but sensed it only for its
negative potential. I had indeed come to that
"time of deadly peril" of which Dr. Jung speaks. I
was shortly to become aware of it myself. The
night after my last hour with her, however, I

dreamt not of peril but of teams of powerful black horses pulling snow plows and dashing about clearing the snow off a railroad yard. A good dream, I thought, and I wrote her about it, hoping it would reassure her. But shortly, within a few days, something else occurred that was so far from my expectation, so far from anything that I had thought in the realm of the possible, that it has taken me the rest of my life to come to terms with it. Since I am convinced that this was the psychic event of which the sonnets were an intuitive foreshadowing, let me introduce the sonnets here and talk about them a little.

A Glimpse of the Center

I. Kneel down, and render up desire, yield up
   Desire, and all the urgency of the day;
   Pride, shame, the upper and the nether stay
   Of this our mortal bearing, render up.
   Here at the cold stone table we must sup
   Our fill of horror; here the poor heart must lay
   Its dearest scruple down at last, nor may
   The shuddering will here set aside the cup.
   Kneel down, and render up desire, for here
   The cup is filled with that beyond desire—
   Beyond our asking and beyond our fear,
   Beyond our dream, the cup is filled with fire.
   And, though the whole world reel, the quiet flame
   Is always, with most constant light, the same.
                                        November 30, 1941

II. O my desire, and of my heart the turning,
    The helm, the home, the pilgrimage, the peace,
    Haven of all hope, and lantern of all learning,
    The lore, the law, the binding, the release—

Into the solid world of time's creating
The everlasting Moment breaking through
Shatters the stone, the steel, the armor-plating,
Shadows the flower, the wing, the sheen, the hue.
These are the phantasms, these the shell, the seeming;
These are the fading and forgotten things;
Under our sun they are but dust and dreaming,
Dust and the recurrent patterns that time brings.
But the eternal Now athwart them gleaming
Gives them their life in the broad beam it flings.

May 14, 1942

III. Hushed in the cradle lies the winter's child,
Submissive to his homely heritage.
Hushed is the unicorn that was so wild
And hushed the transports of his kingly rage.
For his sole baby sake his mother yearned
And bore immensity within her womb;
And he round whom the poles of heaven turned
Accepts the shelter of a narrow room.
When shall the childish hands, at length unclosing,
Reveal the stubborn purpose of his will?
And on what paths of heaven's obscure disposing
Shall his constrained feet walk, unwilling still?
And what redeeming evil, of whose choosing,
Shall pierce her heart who never uttered ill?

May 24, 1943

IV. What the hand shapes, what the hand shapes, is not
His, not the dark, not the unchosen clay
And not the incorruptible pattern; it is not
Of the maker. The maker may betray
His hand in some crease, some wrinkle, but the pot,
Substance and shape, reveals another will,
Not his, not mine, not of the daylight, not
Of night as I know the night. It is still

Awkward by any human measure, still
Ugly, still unacceptable, still cold.
How can we tell so surely that it will
Shine with so clear a grace when we are old?
And how so truly recognize the shrill
Tomorrow's beauty in the stubborn mould?
                                    November 2, 1943

A friend of mine who is a professional poet has
recently made several suggestions for improving
these sonnets. In most instances I agreed with
what she had to say, but I have decided to leave them
in the state in which they were written some
forty years ago. Additionally, she pointed out the
use of *desire* in two quite different senses in the
first and second sonnets. There is nothing I can do
about this; it is the way the inspiration came. I
have since noted the paradox in the second sonnet, where the central value is described as both
destroying and creating. Again, that is the way it
came to me; it expresses a truth beyond logic.

There are a few other things I can say about
the sonnets that may make them more compre-
hensible. The cup in the first sonnet suggests the
symbolism of the Grail, and indeed I had been
much preoccupied with this symbolism in the
early part of my analysis. During that first year I
painted a picture of the Grail procession—the
wailing women, the dying Fisher King, the knights
in armor. So much has now been written about
this that I hardly need say any more. There is, of
course, Mrs. Jung's study of the Grail legend. But I
had come to it by way of Jessie Weston's *From
Ritual to Romance*, which is mentioned in the

notes to T. S. Eliot's *Waste Land* to illustrate the underlying symbolism of the poem. I was much occupied with Eliot in those days. At the time I came to analysis, I already thought I understood *Ash Wednesday,* and I worked hard on *The Waste Land* concurrently with my analytic work, writing in the second year of analysis a paper on Eliot that finally was published years later. The experience described in my first sonnet corresponds to the reductive phase of analysis and has a certain analogy with the phase of purgation in the mystical quest.

The second and third sonnets essentially explain themselves in their depiction of the invocation and the new birth. They are full of references to the medieval poems that had made such an impression on me; some of those references I can see and I am sure there are others that I am unaware of. The heaping up of metaphors in the second sonnet is found over and over again in the Latin poems and I think sometimes in the English. "Lantern of all learning" is so medieval an epithet that I feel I must have borrowed it; but I cannot find it anywhere, so perhaps it is an invention in the medieval spirit. The unicorn of course has been much studied, as for instance in Dr. Jung's writing on alchemy, but the attributes I have given him may have been borrowed from less respectable characters. For instance, the words "that was so wild" occur in a Middle English poem as a description of the "fiend," that is, the devil, and in one of the medieval guild plays on biblical topics that used to be enacted on large wagons. King Herod, if I remember correctly, when he learns that the

Child has escaped the massacre of the innocents, "rageth in the pageant and in the street also"—so it is possible that I borrowed the "kingly rage" from that source, although in my mind's eye the kingly rage of the unicorn is still dignified, while I suspect that the Herod of the mystery plays was looking for laughs.

The fourth sonnet no longer uses the language of the symbolic quest, because that language is no longer relevant. Here the symbolism is low key, down to earth. It describes the daily task, but a task no longer meaningless because it is infused by something that comes not from the hand of the worker, nor entirely from the ego that directs the hand, but "reveals another will." The sonnets were published anonymously in the *Bulletin* of the Analytical Psychology Club in 1948.

The sonnets were a prevision of the subjective event that I have already mentioned and that occurred within a few days of my finally taking leave of Dr. Harding. The juxtaposition of events—the quick transition from the uneasy argument and the unsatisfactory parting to the extraordinary beauty of intellectual vision (which I think is the technical name for what occurred) baffled me for a long time, but was explained for me by a passage in Dr. Edward F. Edinger's *Ego and Archetype* in which he says that the Self is often projected on the analyst. Although at one level I knew this, and had already adumbrated the idea in my second *Bulletin* paper on the group, I did not recognize it in my own case. Strange, how many levels of understanding are required of us. When at any rate the projection was at last successfully withdrawn, after years of struggle, I came to a confrontation with the Self, or to use a term that satisfies me better, with the Other. Such an event, a true experience of the Numinous, occurring as it did to one reared in the most staid and unemotional branch of Protestantism, taught to believe that such things were truly impossible, or if not impossible then certainly abnormal—such an event was truly overwhelming.

I can do no better than to quote from an account which I wrote several years ago as a record for my family:

The climactic event, the real turning point, came a year or so after I had completed the sonnet sequence, I believe in the spring of 1945, and it came in a visitation that all my upbringing and education told me was simply an impossibility—unless of course one was psychotic. We were living in Wayne and I was teaching at Bryn Mawr. It must have been during the college vacation, because I was at home on a Monday afternoon and the children were not around. I lay down for a nap on the living room sofa. I will tell the preliminaries as well as I can after thirty-odd years, since I think they are interesting. I had a dream of levitation; I seemed to be suspended in the air a foot or two above the sofa. But my good Jungian training had emphasized the importance of "keeping my feet on the ground," so, still in the dream, I said to myself, "This will never do," and I managed to pull myself back down to the sofa. There was a further fragment of a dream, something about the beating of wings above and around me. Then I woke up. The experience I then had would have been called hallucinatory by a psychiatrist of the day, perhaps by most today. In the technical language of mysticism (and I use the word in its strictest sense, not in the popular sense of some sort of fuzzy pleasurable contact with the unconscious) it is what is called "intellectual vision." [The Jungian reader must not confuse this medieval use of the word *intellectual,* meaning in the mind, not perceived by the outward senses, with our contemporary use of the word as referring to the thinking function.] That is, I saw nothing unusual with my outward eye, but I nevertheless knew that there was someone else in the room with me. A few feet in front of me and a little to the left stood a numinous figure, and between us was an interchange, a flood, flowing both ways, of love. There were no words, no sound. There was light everywhere. It was the end of March, and everywhere outdoors shrubs were in flower, and indoors and out, the world was flooded with light, the supernal light that so many of the mystics describe and a few of the poets. The vision lasted five days; sometime on Saturday afternoon I had a sense of fatigue, and could sustain it no longer, and it faded. There was no one around to whom I could tell it. Roger [my husband] who is embarrassed and alarmed at the mere mention of religious experience, would have thought me utterly mad, as I surely would have thought anyone mad who told me such a story. Indeed the part of me that still adhered to my rationalist upbringing fully agreed with this point of view. I knew that I was in a precarious situation; that if my ego could manage to annex or engulf the experience I might well be tilted toward psychosis. Yet the experience was so overwhelmingly good that I couldn't mistrust it. I knew that it was important to keep my feet on the ground, to keep my nose to the grindstone. I remember that we entertained Grandmother Foster for two or three days that week. I took her to lunch at the Deanery on the Bryn Mawr campus with that glory blazing all around me. I went to the movies with Roger. I did all the usual things. The thing that I did to help me understand the experience was to get Evelyn Underhill's *Mysticism,* the classic text on the subject, out of the college library and to read the relevant portions over and over for the next year. I realized that some of the medieval poems I had been so innocently handling were written to invoke just such an experience as I had had. (That stuff is still alive, I tell you.)

Evelyn Underhill's book was the chief help I got in understanding this tremendous experience. It was of crucial importance to me to know that what had come so suddenly into my life was not something totally new and unknown, but that such an event had a name and had been experienced and understood centuries ago. None of my various mentors understood it at all. I wrote at once to Dr. Harding, though without giving her a full description; she replied immediately that such an occurrence was almost certainly to be mistrusted. This was, of course, the good orthodox analyst's response. Indeed, to understand it for what it really was, she would have had to reverse her opinion of much of my development for the past several years, and she was a woman who did not reverse herself easily. Within the next few years I mentioned it to Dr. Nordfeldt and subsequently to Mrs. Wickes, one of the earliest established of the Jungian analysts, with whom I did some work related to my first job in a child guidance clinic. From both of them I got a sympathetic hearing, but no real understanding; to them

such a thing seemed a sort of psychic curiosity, a
side issue, not really related to the business of development, while for me it was the most important thing that had ever happened to me. So I was
left to live with it and gradually to come to terms
with it, and that process, as I have said, has taken
the rest of my life.

Some of the people who have read this account
in the course of the preparation of this essay have
asked urgently for a more complete description.
What else happened? Were you able to sleep? Did
the experience alter your relations with your family? Above all, just *how* did it change your life?
But the essence of the matter is that the experience
was quite simple—overwhelming but simple—and
yet so at odds with twentieth-century thinking, at
least as I have experienced it. So far as I can remember, I slept as usual. I went about my daily
business as usual, though I was staggering, metaphorically speaking, from wonder at what was
happening to me. I had been an imaginative child
from the beginning, and I had had an early training in concealing my inner life from those around
me. In the practical sense, my relation to my family was unaffected. I didn't start speaking with
them differently, dealing with them differently.
But I saw them now—my husband, my two sons,
my daughter, our housekeeper, my mother-in-law,
who visited us that week and my relation to
whom had always caused me some anxiety and
some effort, my students, all the people I dealt
with from day to day—and indeed everything
around us, our house, the flowering world outside,

the college where I worked, the commuter train I rode—all these people and things I saw now *sub specie eternitatis*, bathed in that supernal light. Similar experiences are described in Evelyn Underhill's book, for mine resembles in some ways the typical "conversion" experience, though I think it is not identical, and this similarity was a stabilizing factor; other people had known the same feelings, had seen the same light—in fact, the common metaphor in our daily speech, "to see the light," often jocosely used, must have come ultimately from just such experiences in the old days when they were still recognized as valid. The reader who asks, "Just *how* did it change your life?" must see, I think, that even though such a vision has faded, life can never return to its former pattern. My central experience had been similar to that of some of the poets, a single temporary vision, time-limited and not to be compared with those of the religious mystics who live constantly in contemplation of the Unseen. But it altered my life permanently, and that value of which I was permitted an awareness in those few days has for me transcended all others. A philosopher nephew of mine said that in the course of our lives, God is glimpsed "now here, now here, and now here." He is speaking for those for whom God is not mediated by traditional religious symbolism. In other words, that "autonomous complex" (in Jung's words) which is God's manifestation, the central complex of the human psyche, that spark, "that of God" which the Quakers say we all carry within us, is projected by the small child to the parents at first, and then here and there, and if its progress is not channeled by traditional religion, mostly to other people—often, as in my case, to a "mentor"— but by some temperaments to the great blossoming world with its diurnal light. In some temperaments the ego claims it and the *I* becomes all important, and this tendency may be symbolized by our curious habit in English of capitalizing the first person singular. In a vision such as mine— still a projection, I assume, for what else are we humans capable of?—that central value reveals itself detached from human and material objects, and shining with its own light. When that happens, it assumes the central position in the psyche, and, to use Jung's metaphor again, the ego revolves around it as the earth revolves around the sun. Any work that I did thereafter was done not as a personal achievement, but as an offering to that Other whom I now recognized. There is no longer so much of the feeling that *I* do this and this (*I* live my life, *I* pursue my career) as that life lives itself through me. This last again is Jung's phrase, but it was also my experience. When this happens, there is a true alteration of the psychic structure. Many other people, I know, have come to this development by other paths, usually and less dangerously within the confines of traditional religion. I was extraordinarily fortunate in finding Evelyn Underhill's book when I did. The support of human understanding is so important in such an encounter, and that I lacked. The fact that I found the right book at the right time, and that I was so well anchored in the real world, with husband, children, and students to whom I was daily responsible, I think kept me stable. The over-rational Western ego is terribly vulnerable.

I have described my experience as "intellectual vision," which is a term I found in Evelyn Underhill. It is part of St. Teresa's classification of visions, and it refers to those in which nothing is seen with the outer eye, nor even by the vivid pictorial imagination of the inner eye; one "knows" in some obscure way that the figure is there. Even the suggestion of spatial placement, "a few feet in front of me and a little to the left," may have disappeared after the first moments; memory fails me on this point. But I knew that I was "companioned" and that the Companion was numinous. After five days the vision faded—but not wholly. I have had ever since an intuitive awareness of being "companioned." That numinous figure is still there, I know, and it is the deficiency of my vision that prevents me from seeing it. As it is there for everyone, I am convinced, as it was for Arjuna, whose charioteer had been the divine Krishna all along, but to whom the god revealed himself only when the battle was imminent. So yes, surely my relation to my family was affected—it could not have been otherwise, and so was my relation to the work I did in the world; but it is not easy to describe the nature and extent of its effect. What does impress me is that gradually my imaginative life and my practical life merged and flowed in one channel, and such of my work as was effective, such as took root in the real world, arose from this merging.

I don't think this centering experience so much enhanced what I had insistently called my "creativity"—my tendency to dip into the unconscious and come back with some alluring picture or bright idea (this I had from childhood and by nature)—but what it did was to enhance my reality sense; it gave body to my intuitions. The Jungian reader will recognize here that I am describing the emergence of the "inferior functions," but I will try to refrain from being too didactic. I was by nature highly intuitive and imaginative, forgetful and impractical, with my feet a bit off the ground, but with a pretty good "secondary thinking function" that turned me in college into a bit of an intellectual. The centering process put me in better touch with what Jung would have called my "inferior functions," feeling and sensation, and without them my bright ideas might have remained oftener just bright ideas. There are geniuses who seem to me to bypass this process; they seem to translate the messages from the unconscious directly into action or expression; in them the integration sometimes seems to take place in the work and not necessarily in the personality. But I was one of the plodders.

Meditation

It is important that the vision came to me at the height of the "mid-life crisis." And now what I want to share with the reader is something of my speculation. It is the residue of my years of brooding on the subject, a mere meditation, not a study; but such as it is, it is my legacy, and I here offer it. The vision of a Center implies also the more mundane centering involved in the archetype of wholeness, that archetype relevant to the stage of life in which I found myself. The old topic of the "stages of life" has been newly and fruitfully studied in our time; among many that have influenced me I would mention Erik Erikson's now famous *Childhood and Society*, published more than thirty years ago, and that recent study of young and middle adulthood by Daniel Levinson and his research team at Yale, *The Seasons of a Man's Life*. But the way in which biological and emotional changes at crucial stages are accompanied by the appearance of the archetypes relevant to each stage has not been much observed, and I fervently hope that someone will undertake the task.

Vision is an impressive communication from the deep unconscious. But there are lesser ways in which the unconscious speaks to us: for instance, dreams, fantasy, play. Dreams, if we are attentive to them, furnish usually a day-to-day commentary, a running guide. They come mostly from the personal unconscious and seem to respond to the question, "What does the unconscious think about what is happening right now?" Once in a while a more urgent dream, presumably from a deeper level, seems to fill a larger function, minatory or prophetic. Fantasy and play involve the ego in their operations, and they seem to offer a way of creating the future, of working out the personal destiny. Looking back at my younger self, I am impressed that the important fantasies came at the biological turning points, and surely this must be so for other people too. I am not speaking of the kind of fantasy that provides a mere diversion, an "escape" from everyday reality, though this too has its uses. But wholesale pursuit of this kind of fantasy, or the more deceptive allure of "meaningful" thought not anchored in reality, can become pretty empty and in extreme cases dangerous. The achievement of Jung and his followers, and of like-minded people not strictly Jungian, in the study of myth and symbol and in the assessing of relevant data—their labor, that is, on the glossary of the archetypical language—offers a measure of redemption for our machine-minded culture. The Bollingen Foundation has published not only Jung's collected works, but those of many people laboring in this field, notably Joseph Campbell's, and it has supported the development of the Archive for Research in Archetypical Symbolism, which has now become the property of the C. G. Jung Foundation in New York. Contact with this material is a heady experience, and it seems to me that the impact on the development of the individual, the effects of the two different kinds of fantasy (or in the words of the romantic poets, of imagination and fantasy) have not yet been much studied. Reading the literature, I sometimes find myself spinning around in the empyrean, with no point of reference on earth. Jung himself touches on this problem occasionally, but for all his profound contact with the unconscious he was himself so well anchored in the real world that it seems not to have concerned him much. The danger to the analysand is that one lives an analysis rather than a life. But as I read the Jungian journals, I think there are signs now that this problem is being considered, at least by some people.

The thought that I am trying to sketch here—alas, I have not the physical ability to pursue the data that would flesh it out—is that as we proceed from stage to stage in life we proceed under the tutelage of one psychic image after another (I am not saying anything new here, but changing the emphasis), that these archetypes appear to us as the psychic counterpart of instincts at the points

when biological change is rapid and is accompanied by a rush of psychic energy, and that we are
not ready—most of us are not ready, at least—to
encounter the central Archetype until, at mid-life,
we have more or less satisfactorily lived through
the other encounters—remembering always that
life does not require perfection of us, only a good
try. The numinous Archetype is there from the beginning, it is the "ground of the soul," but it is
usually not yet experienced as something separate
in itself; it is implicated with other people and
things usually for the first half of life. Until then,
other archetypes dominate the field of interest. In
the Oedipal stage, we begin to recognize our common destiny—to experience and work on the archetype of Woman in relation to Man, or of Man
in relation to Woman. It is the first significant
step away from the parents, who are the godlike
figures in our lives. We work on it, mostly in
secret, all the years of our childhood, and it
springs to life again in adolescence and is usually
realized in actual fact. But in adolescence, something new enters the picture, more strongly for
some than for others. Erik Erikson has described
the struggle for identity during this period; and for
some people at this age, perhaps a small minority,
it would seem that the unconscious imposes an
additional individual task, presents an idea, a
cause, an image, to which each is impelled to devote himself. This too is an archetypical experience, and it seems to be the channel through
which social change comes about; young people
are its carriers. It seems impossible to exaggerate

this fact, which is scarcely recognized and hardly studied at all. Nobody has described a sudden biological change at mid-life (age thirty-seven to forty-three by Levinson's definition), but this has now been defined as a crisis period, and my guess is that biologists will sooner or later discover subtle biochemical changes of some sort, as the zenith of adulthood is passed and the course is set toward death. At any rate, it is only at this time, it would seem, that for most people a direct encounter with the central Archetype is possible. In the meantime, much wisdom has usually been projected to a friend or co-worker, usually older and usually but not always of the same sex, and it is only with the loosening of this bond, its transformation or termination, that an intrapsychic confrontation with the Other becomes possible. Levinson does not go so far as this, but it was my experience, and I would suspect it has been that of others. It is not always explicitly recognized; it may be only vaguely understood. There may be a search for wholeness. Values and pursuits long neglected may be rediscovered and vigorously pursued. In natures for whom a more explicit encounter is a necessity, there may be a search, going on into the fifties, for some special formulation, philosophic, scientific, or philanthropic, which will somehow allay one's restlessness. Let me go back and fill out this outline a little.

Anyone observing the play of young children will regard it in most cases as sturdy and purposive, "auto-therapeutic" in some instances, to use Erikson's word, because coping with distressing

events is one of the functions of play, but more
often it is the trying on of roles, or more especially a working over, with zest and pleasure, of a
seemingly permanently chosen role—one's own
kind of manhood, one's own kind of womanhood—
and of those feelings and activities that go with it.
It would seem that the role is usually chosen in
the preschool years, and this choice seems like the
setting of a task for the imagination, which will
work at it, often underground and unobserved,
until the next great turning point is reached and
the archetypes speak again.

Margaret McFarland, of the University of Pittsburgh, has made voluminous and systematic observations of the play of the same group of children
in her own neighborhood over many years; they are
unique so far as I know and I hope they will be
published some day. She has kindly allowed me to
read some of her notes, and I remember among
them a charming play sequence of a little girl of
five, staging a wedding procession with a set of
small dolls. The little girl doll and the mother doll
have to alternate as the bride; the veil, I seem to
remember, made out of Kleenex, is passed from
one to the other, and because the child cannot—
cannot yet—work out this knotty problem of who
is really the bride, between the claims of desire
and reality, the dolls are finally all pushed over on
the floor with the proclamation, "Everybody has to
fall down," and the game ends in chaos. But she
will work it out, in many games alone or with her
friends, whether the observer is present or not, and
later observations show she has done so. The con-

sistency of imagination over the years is truly impressive. I recall one such game from my own early childhood, which must have come from a slightly later age than that of Dr. McFarland's little friend of the wedding procession, and which I suppose I remember because I shared it with friends, and this made it more real. Unquestioningly it had had its origin in the Oedipal years, but my earliest memories of it, and the earliest records, for there were records, in the form of maps, pictures, little books, and so forth, all dated from the years when I could read and write. Marion H., my life-long friend, used to recount how when we first met, at the age of about ten, I pulled the map of an imaginary ocean out of my pocket and invited her to draw in an island, or rather two islands. My two, the islands of Caw and Blue, were already drawn in, along with various others contributed by my brother and by other friends. She drew in her two, the islands of Fi-foo and Kay. These were attached by an isthmus. As for my two, Blue, the second one, had an arctic climate, the people lived in igloos, and it was largely neglected. Caw was the important one. On the island of Caw, the culture was very simple; houses and costumes were unadorned and more or less uniform; the technology was within my grasp. Children were ready to marry at about the age of six. I was married to a boy named Elratinga who wore his hair in a "Dutch cut," the style then for little boys. We had nine children, including twins and triplets, each of whom appeared in the middle of the night, "out of the nowhere into the here," as the rhyme said.

56

Some of the little books that lay around my parents' home for years, written in a slightly disguised script, were baby books for various of these children. About Marion's island of Fi-foo, I remember less, except that the inhabitants wore middy blouses and bloomers, the athletic costume for girls at that time. What the adventures were that kept the fantasies going for Marion and me I have totally forgotten, but during the year that she spent in Rome, when we must have been twelve or thirteen, we wrote long letters back and forth, illustrated with paintings, about the doings of our respective islands. One feature of the land of Fi-foo I do remember. It had among its inhabitants a witch named Paura (pronounced "Pa-oo-ra"; it means *fear* in Italian). Marion at the end of her life spent long years in a nursing home, far gone with a wasting nerve disease. Those of us who knew her best recognized that in an obscure form she had always had it, and that it had hampered her always in the full living of her life. Is it too fantastic to see in this early witch a premonition of this fate, a hereditary affliction apparently passed on by her mother? In spite of the illness of her old age, Marion always recognized her friends. I usually went up to see her in company with her closest friend, Marion M., who visited every day, and often one or another of us would remind her of our childhood games, and this made her laugh. So we three old girls sat there chuckling together over those faraway times.

Already at an early age, it seems, an image emerges, of Woman in relation to Man, partly called into being by observation of life around the child, partly because the archetype, the psychic counterpart of the instinctual development of the Oedipal years, has touched the little girl and made her aware of her destiny. The child responds and begins to enact her role, in play and dream and fantasy.

You may ask what this has to do with a visionary experience at mid-life. When we are children, the Self, the Other, is ordinarily implicated with the powerful and divine-seeming parents. Some of this numinosity separates itself from the parents and casts a golden sheen at moments in our fantasy play. I can remember that when I was six or seven somebody had given me an empty candy box to play with. I had cut little windows and a door in it, and when it was turned upside down on the floor it made a little house. In those days candy boxes came with a trimming of lace paper along the sides, and I had torn off the paper and pasted it on either side of the windows to make lace curtains. Lying on the floor I peered in at the door. The gas light above cast the shadow of the little lace curtains on the floor, and I was seized with what I can only describe as a sort of ecstasy. There was all of nest-building in this feeling—the woman's passion for what Erikson calls inner space—and all of aesthetic experience, for the pattern of the little lace curtains on the floor was really beautiful. I recognized such a moment of ecstasy in my daughter when at a comparable age she found that her pet hamster had given birth to a litter of tiny pink naked babies. "Oh!" she kept exclaiming, "I have *never* seen anything so cute."

These important moments come and go, and
mostly we fail to notice them, but these are the
times when, as Jung says, the archetypes "tap us
on the shoulder." They occur especially, it seems,
at the nodes of development; at the Oedipal period, or after that period and referring back to it;
at adolescence, or referring back to it; at mid-life;
and I believe and hope, in old age. Surely this is
the sequence of the long, long struggle to wrest
the intuited image of God from its first objects
and to invest it elsewhere, successively, in other
objects, each of whom will be revealed in time to
be, however dearly loved, not fully adequate. A few
children do seem to have a more direct awareness
of the transcendental, something like true mystical
experiences in childhood. Wordsworth is the famous example of this:

> The earth, and every common sight
>   To me did seem
> Apparell'd in celestial light.
>   ("Ode: Intimations of Immortality")

And at least two of the seventeenth-century
poets describe comparable experiences. For these
God is seen, or felt, in nature or in the world
about. The most moving description of this childhood experience is Thomas Traherne's, written toward the end of his life (he died in mid-life, at
about thirty-eight).

I was entertained like an angel with the works of God
in the peace of Eden; heaven and earth did sing my Cre-
ator's praise, and could not make more melody to Adam
than to me. Is it not strange that an infant should be

heir of the whole world, and see those mysteries which the books of the learned never unfold? . . . The corn was orient and immortal wheat which never should be reaped nor was ever sown. I thought it had stood from everlasting to everlasting. The dust and stones of the street were precious as gold: the gates were at first the end of the world. The green trees when I saw them first through one of the gates transported and ravished me; their sweetness and unusual beauty made my heart to leap, and almost mad with ecstasy, they were such strange and wonderful things. The men! Oh what venerable and reverend creatures did the aged seem! Immortal cherubims! And young men glittering and sparkling angels, and maids strange seraphic pieces of life and beauty! Boys and girls tumbling in the street were moving jewels: I knew not that they were born or should die. But all things abided eternally as they were in their proper places. Eternity was manifest in the light of the Day, and something infinite behind everything appeared, which talked with my expectation and moved my desire. (*Centuries of Meditations*)

Or in the words of Traherne's slightly older contemporary, Henry Vaughan,

> Happy those early days when I
> Shin'd in my angel-infancy!   ("The Retreat")

It is a pity we do not have more exact ages for these experiences, but the designations "infancy," "early childhood" are suggestions at least of the period before children were sent to school. For each of these poets capable of describing such early experiences, there must have been others who failed to leave records. Phyllis Greenacre, one of the most acute of the Freudian observers of early development, has noted other signs of what might be called religious feeling in certain children and differentiates one kind from another. "It is very striking how many creative people describe memories of experiences of revelation, awe, or some kind of transcendental states in childhood and how regularly this is placed at the age of four or five. But there is another component of religious feeling from early childhood which involves not so much of ecstasy in which fear gives some special intensity, but rather a sense of fusion with the outer world in a state of mutual permeability, sometimes described as an *oceanic feeling.* . . . A sense of special lightness or airiness may pervade either of these subjective states producing an illusion of flying or of floating." ("The Family Romance of the Artist," p. 34). The writer believes these feelings are derived from the early experience of nursing, but this reductive explanation, perhaps accurate, need not trouble us. The religious feeling has to seize on whatever metaphor is available to it.

Freudian analysts describe a "feeling of awe," seemingly of religious intensity, that sometimes occurs with the child's first glimpse of the father's penis, and I find such observations convincing. Perhaps this is how phallus worship originated in the first place. But are we to think of the penis as the primary factor in the situation, so that the religious awe is reduced to anatomical observation? Or is this an early instance in that sequence of events in which God is glimpsed "now here, now here, and now here?" If I may be so irreverent, Freudian psychology, with all its important values, might be thought of from one point of view as a late-Western appearance of phallus worship.

The sexual feelings are rearoused at puberty. But they have never entirely gone away. Observations of children's play suggest that they are there throughout the so-called latency period, though often disguised and more subdued. I remember a presentation by Dr. Ray Birdwhistell, the student of body language. He showed us two films of latency-age children at play, boys playing with boys, girls with girls, as is so regularly the case at that age. Two little boys were engaged in that ubiquitous sport of "wrestling." At one point the camera was halted and we studied the picture. One of the little boys, laughing, was holding the other down in what might have been interpreted as a mock sexual encounter. Presently he would let him get up and the game would begin all over. In the other film the pair of little girls were digging worms to go fishing. They had accumulated quite a canful when on an impulse one of the little girls began to pelt the other with the worms. Again the camera stopped. The child who was being pelted was shielding herself as well as she could, half turned away from her tormentor, thighs tight together, one shoulder raised, eyes shut. The other youngster, laughing, stood a-straddle with knees bent like a young gunman, one arm raised in the act of flinging a worm. So the drama is played out unconsciously, over and over, sex and aggression mingled, but playfully.

All this we know, and with puberty it all becomes more conscious and the players begin to

search for their true counterparts. But the archetype that dominates adolescence, as Erik Erikson
has demonstrated so vividly (though he does not
use the term *archetype*), is that of the individual.
The crisis of adolescence, in his view, is the identity crisis; and our collective agreement is so great
that his term has entered the common speech and
is used and misused constantly. For some adolescents, I imagine, the personal identity develops
quietly out of those images and aspirations encountered in childhood play. The once-little girl
who has finally sorted out her feelings about
father and mother and who encounters in real life
her own Elratinga or whatever his name is, the
one who corresponds somehow to her archetype of
the Man, who pretty well fits the projection she is
prepared to make — such a girl may have found her
identity and her career as wife and mother. But
adolescence is another time of proliferating fantasy, an exploration of feelings, urges, and ideals,
and upon some young people the unconscious
seems to impose a task different from the average,
perhaps even indicating the destiny, even the
future life-work of the individual. More than that:
by this channel tomorrow's values make their way
into society. The changes in our culture seem to
be filtered in from the collective unconscious
through its adolescents; they are the natural revo-
lutionaries. "Bliss was it in that dawn to be alive,"
Woodsworth wrote of the France of the early revo-
lution, "But to be young was very heaven" (*Prelude*,
bk. 11). "It seems to me," writes Kurt Eissler in
"Creativity and Adolescence," "that all cultural

achievements by great minds are in a direct genetic connection with their adolescence. Indeed, it may be questioned whether true original values can be found after adolescence. . . . Apart from the new formations created out of the old ones, new contents are channelled into the unconscious. It is my impression that during adolescence a huge stock of highly cathected imagery accumulates that serves as a store for the rest of life. Creative minds, I imagine, have only to reach back into that store in order to obtain new imagery, new problems, new tasks" (p. 511). This is not to suggest, I believe, that every rebellious adolescent is contributing deathless ideas to the world. The quotation applies to the very creative person. Surely however there must be many of middling sensitivity to whom the urgent concerns of their time present themselves in fantasy form. How many women of my generation, I wonder, experienced, as I did, a fantasy of the new woman, the Woman as Person? My fantasy, rather fragmentary and incomplete as it happened, was a *Bildungsroman,* and concerned my upbringing in a community of women into which I was kidnapped in mid-adolescence; it was my education at the hands of the Mothers. My community of women corresponded closely to that described in *Herland,* the story by an advocate of women's rights, Charlotte Perkins Gilman, which I should say is itself an account of a fantasy experience. I had never seen her book (published in 1915) until it was reprinted recently, but my fantasy came out of the same climate. My mother and grandmother were suffragists.

Both had been teachers and both had suffered from the fact that marriage had forced them to give up a much-loved profession. They couldn't have both, and each chose marriage and motherhood, the deeper need; but each of them had much in addition to give, and no opportunity to give it. There must have been many Herlands in existence, most unrecorded. I recognized Charlotte Gilman's serene, grave women at once, although mine were not always serene and grave—they had some humor and were capable of anger on occasion. But the archetype is appearing everywhere now, though it is sometimes distorted in ways that make me shudder. Charlotte Gilman's women are not hostile to men, as her story shows. In fact they watch with benevolent interest while three young men, who have blundered into Herland in their new flying machine, gradually attach themselves to three of the young women. It simply happened that a group of women, accidentally marooned without men but having fortunately discovered a method of parthenogenesis, had been able to develop their own values and their own culture. Herland is a Utopia, as was my realm of women. Separation and secrecy were necessary, in her fantasy and mine, lest the woman-values be overwhelmed by those of the much larger world outside. The archetype they serve is that of the free woman, which is entering the awareness of all of us and taking hold of the imagination much as Rousseau's vision of the free youth took root in the imagination of the eighteenth century and has dominated education ever since:

Come my happy, my lovable pupil. . . . He comes, and I feel at his approach a movement of joy which I see him share. . . . His figure, his bearing, his countenance proclaim assurance and contentment; health shines from his face, his firm steps give him an air of vigor; his complexion, still delicate without being washed out, has no effeminate softness; the air and the sun have already put on it the honorable imprint of his sex; his muscles, still rounded, begin to show some signs of their nascent features; his eyes, which are not yet animated by the fire of sentiment, at least have all their native serenity; long sorrows have not darkened them, unending tears have not lined his cheeks. See in his movements, quick but sure, the vivacity of his age, the firmness of independence, and the experience of much exercise. His aspect is open and free but not insolent or vain. . . . There is no need to say to him, "Lift your head." Neither shame nor fear ever caused him to lower it. (*Emile*, p. 159)

I have not seen an equivalent literary expression of the Woman as Person, but surely there is one somewhere, or there will be. More than a half-century ago, I recall commenting in a paper written for the Shakespeare class in graduate school on the two classes of women the scholars were then discerning in his work. They distinguished the Amazons, those female characters who took matters into their own hands and thereby furthered the action, like Juliet, even at age fourteen, or Lady Macbeth in a very different way, and the non-Amazons, like Ophelia and Desdemona. I had already read a little Jung, and I suggested that the latter type, the lovely but rather pale and passive women, were typical figments of

the male imagination, whereas in the so-called
Amazonian characters, the poet had got inside the
woman's skin and had presented a real human
being. The Shakespeare professor, dear good man,
wrote in the margin of my paper in genuine baffle-
ment, "What does this mean?" I don't think any
English professor would miss my meaning today.
The archetype of the free woman, as I have said,
must be ubiquitous now among women; it
emerges here and there, whether it is realized as a
conscious fantasy or not. On those to whom it appears it imposes a task, and like other such tasks
it spans the generations; those of us now living
will not see it completed.

My fantasy of the mothers was incomplete,
and my education among them was incomplete.
They lived in a fortified, stockaded community
somewhere in the wilds of Canada, where in those
days before airplanes, they had managed to live
undiscovered by the male-dominated world about
them. The visual imagery is very detailed still in
my mind, down to the brick of the fireplaces and
the grain of the wooden tables; the appearance and
personality of each of the major characters is
clear, each identity is distinct, but I never devised
names for any of them. My foster mother in that
community was a violinist and a maker of violins,
and from her I learned to be a good musician; I
had some aptitude and that part was easy. But the
other, subtler things that she and the others had
to teach me I never could fully grasp. There was a
kind of solidity and integrity about these women —
quite apart from the fact that they were strong

and active—which women who measure themselves against the requirements of their masculine counterparts cannot achieve. I could not grasp it fully, and I do not see it in the faces of those who demand women's rights most insistently. But it is in the unconscious, and it will be articulated, I am convinced, somewhere and by somebody.

In the upheaval of adolescence too there sometimes come glimpses of a transcendental value. I am not aware of any descriptions of continuous more-or-less mystical experiences occurring at adolescence that parallel those recalled from their early years by the three poets I have cited. But more fleeting awareness is often experienced in connection with nature—the view from a mountain top, the sight of a starry sky; and in most young people such events are seized upon, innocently enough, by the ego and appear as ideals— hopes and dreams for the individual, experienced for instance, as a member of my family puts it, "climbing alone in the mountains where the period of solitude and withdrawal and contemplation gives way to a rush of enthusiasm and anticipation for the future." In some cases the ego is subordinated and the feeling is a religious one, as in the following communication about an experience when the writer was thirteen: "I felt a presence, as if the whole moonlit sky was watching me. I felt as if I had been peeled out of a hiding place and there was no place to run to. It was not very cold out, but I shivered uncontrollably. I was scared, and yet I was happy, because I now knew that there was more to the world and the universe

than I had thought before. It is very hard to completely describe this sensation, but it stayed with
me until I woke up the next morning." A less
fearful but more overwhelming experience of a
thirteen-year-old is described in the biography of
the seventeenth-century French Jesuit Jean-Joseph
Surin: "One day, as he was attending Vespers, his
heart found itself suddenly flooded with a heavenly
joy that obliged him to sit down as his body could
not support it. He had a supernatural light which
revealed to him in an ineffable manner the gran-
deur of the essence of God. All divine attributes
were manifested to him." A reminiscence of a contemporary of mine tells of a less dramatic conversion experience at a slightly later age. The young
man in question had been taken by his parents to
religious revival meetings in the small town in
which he grew up, but he had not been able to experience conversion in a way satisfactory to himself. Later, in college—this would have been in the
early twenties—he went to another series of revival meetings, "I attended them partly," he writes,
"because I had some doubts about my status as a
Christian. When you are in college you do some
things that might put a strain on your code of
morality. The meeting on that particular night
somehow really got to me and I returned to my
room afterward in a troubled state of mind. After
some thought it seemed natural for me to kneel
down by my bed and in silent prayer ask sincerely
for inner strength and spiritual guidance in my
college life. I was so absorbed and intent that I
lost complete awareness of my surroundings: I

have no idea of how long I was in this state of mind but I remember clearly that eventually I sensed a combination of elation, assurance, and complete peace of mind. I was satisfied and I was glad that I had done it. It was as if someone had been searching desperately for a lost valuable and suddenly there it was!!" There must be many such stories of adolescent religious experience; it is just that in my ultra-rational environment I have not often heard of them.

We have only just discovered that major period of emotional upheaval that comes at mid-life. In fact, not many generations have passed since life was over for most people before or soon after what we now think of as mid-life. A few individuals lived into their seventies and eighties, but not many. Shakespeare seems to have regarded himself as an old man in his late forties, when he gave up the stage business, bought a fine house in his home town (he was one of the few poets to make money at his craft), and became a retired citizen, to enjoy, one hopes "that which should accompany old age / As honour, love, obedience, troops of friends." He had written Prospero and Lear into his later plays, and he died at fifty-three, an age when many of my younger contemporaries are still struggling to realize the insights of mid-life. We are only beginning to think of mid-life as a chronological middle. But at that time there is another emotional upheaval, an enforced change of point of view, and another archetype to come to terms with, and that the most urgent of all. Some of us have had glimpses of it along the way, some not. I have tried to describe how I encountered this crisis, for I think it is an important example, and in this matter we are all at the merest beginning of learning.

Recently when I visited the C. G. Jung Foundation in New York, the librarian put into my hands a newly acquired book which she said might interest me. This was a book of photographs of wall paintings from the Villa of the Mysteries in a suburb of Pompeii, excavated later than the city itself. A typescript commentary by a Swiss Jungian, Linda Fierz-David, and another by Esther Harding, are also in the library, and greatly illuminate the paintings. There are many other, non-Jungian, commentaries on these pictures, as I was to discover later. The murals, in themselves and in the light of such scholarly commentary as I have been able to find, speak to me somewhat as follows. They appear to represent a Dionysian initiation ritual for women, or for a particular woman, a woman's search for personhood and for an ultimate value in that particular period of the Roman Empire when, we are told, women briefly had a degree of freedom and an access to education that (except for a few rare individuals) they were to lose under the Christian church and not to enjoy again for many centuries. The pictures show an initiation ceremony in which human beings, and in particular the initiate, interact with mythical beings until a climax is reached in a revelation of the sacred phallus. In the first picture to the left of the door as one enters, a woman (some commentators describe her as a self-contained young matron, and she looks the part) stands before a priestess, one hand on her hip and the other lifting her garment slightly away from her breast in what is perhaps a ritual gesture. The priestess is seated, and at her knee, with her hand on his shoulder, a naked little boy seems to read aloud from a scroll, the initial instructions, presumably, for the rite. Both the priestess and the little boy have unusual expressions, the child perhaps anxious, the priestess somewhat stern. In the second picture a woman, presumably the same woman, with her cloak now girded around her hips, carries a dish containing a large cake, perhaps an offering, toward a table. A priestess sits at this table with her back to the viewer, and there are two attendants, one of whom pours a libation from a small pitcher. Having sacrified to the gods, the woman now seems to enter the world of the Roman unconscious peopled by lesser deities of half-human, half-animal form. In the next picture a silenus, that amiable dirty old man of classical myth, recognizable by his pointed animal ears, stands with one foot on a stone or platform, his garment slipping below his rotund tummy, and sings and plays on a lyre. Behind him sit two panisks, again partially human creatures with animal ears; one of them is female, and she suckles a little kid which stands before her. Beside them a small he-goat stands alertly and stares out at the viewer. All this seems peaceful and pastoral enough, but in the next picture we see the woman again, and now she is frightened—or is she already possessed? She is clearly in flight, right out of the picture and

into the room. Her cloak, which she has again
flung over her, billows out behind her, and one
foot extends beyond the painted frame of the picture. Her expression is one of anxiety—or is she
already possessed by the god and rushing off to
participate in the mysteries? What has got into
her is probably explained by the next picture,
around the corner of the room. Here a silenus
holds a jar, tilting it so that its bottom faces the
viewer, as he simultaneously raises his head and
looks at the fleeing woman. Behind the silenus is
a young faun with animal ears, bending over and
peering with raised eyebrows into the cauldron.
Above them another faun leans forward with what
is described as a sly expression, almost a leer, and
holds out toward the viewer a terrifying silenus
mask, dark, bearded, its mouth open. What all this
means we can only guess. Something has happened to shatter the woman's self-possession—she
is terrified or possessed, or both. Next comes the
dominant picture of the series, unfortunately dam-
aged because the upper wall has been broken. This
is a large representation of Dionysus and Adriadne,
the god at ease, half reclining against his partner.

Now it becomes evident that our intiate has
not run away permanently. For she reappears,
kneeling to the right of the great deity. She seems
to have taken part in a torch-light procession; the
heavy-looking torch, now extinguished, is cradled
on her shoulder. Her hair is covered by a sort of
cap. Before her is the sacred winnowing basket,
and with her free hand she begins to raise the
cloth which covers it, to behold, we can only sup-

pose, the sacred phallus within. It would seem
that she has completed the initiation rite.

But now comes the denouement, and a most
curious one. To the right of the woman appears a
dark-winged figure described by the commentators
as an angel, the edge of her garment slightly curled
by her rapid descent. Her eyes are on the kneeling
woman. She holds her left hand, palm out, toward
the woman in a gesture of aversion, as if forbid-
ding something. In her right hand she carries a
whip. And in the next picture, around the corner,
the chastisement is about to begin. The woman
kneels, her head in the lap of the priestess, who
now, for whatever reason, wears the same sort of
cap that the woman wore in the preceding picture.
The priestess with one hand supports the initiate's
disheveled head in a gesture described by one of
the commentators as "almost maternal," while
with her other hand she pushes aside the garment
from the initiate's naked back, on which the whip
is about to descend. It seems as though the initiate has done something wrong and has to be punished for it. Perhaps she has erred in lifting the
covering of the sacred winnowing basket; the mystery should not have been revealed; or perhaps she
has incurred a psychic inflation, which must be
corrected. It seems, however, that this episode is
not an aberration; it has parallels in other representations of the mystery cult; the initiate begins
to raise the cloth and is stopped by a supernatural
figure, an angel or a nymph, with upraised hand.
In some versions there is instead a robed female
figure, perhaps a goddess, who seems to turn her

back and walk away, and there is one picture in which the kneeling woman with the sacred basket before her seems to clutch at the garment of this robed figure as if to hold her back. At any rate, in our pictures the whip looks very heavy and the chastisement seems a dreadful one, but all appears right at the end. Two women, one naked and holding aloft a pair of small cymbals, one richly dressed and carrying a thyrsis, engage in a ritual dance. The beautifully dressed one is considered to be our initiate.

There are two more pictures; opinions seem to differ as to whether they are part of the series. In the next one a woman (our woman?) sits in a chair while her hair is dressed by a maid. A naked cupid stands beside them and holds up a mirror into which the maid gazes while she works, while her mistress looks out toward the viewer. The final picture is a portrait, and a most impressive one. A woman (our initiate? the mother superior of the cult?) sits in a chair, one arm supported by a cushion on the arm of the chair. She is beautiful, though not young; she has an expression of great serenity. And so ends the series.

The mere existence, at that date—some time before the eruption of Vesuvius in 79 A.D.—of an independent women's mystery cult, in itself stirs the imagination. But the really extraordinary feature of the series is the irruption of the "angel" toward the end of the series. My theologian brother-in-law, to whom I applied for information about angels, suggested, I am sure accurately, that this figure is not really an angel but is one of the Erinyes, the

Punishers, who pursue important wrongdoers.
This jibes with the fact that this figure is clearly
female, while angels (who aren't part of Graeco-
Roman mythology anyway) usually appear as men.
She also wears the short tunic and the hunting
boots that are characteristic of the Erinyes, who
were originally huntresses. But it is what this figure is saying to the woman that is important. It
seems to me that what the Erinys, with her upraised hand, forbids is the worship of the phallus.
Rather hard on the woman, who has gone through
the long initiation, the offering of the cake, the
confrontation with strange supernatural beings,
the torch-light procession, only to be told she is
worshipping the wrong god. But in the end, having
been corrected, she dances with what must be a
naked female divinity; we are told by the commentators that nakedness equals divinity.

These pictures did indeed, as the librarian sur-
mised, arouse my interest, because they resonated
so strongly with the unfinished business of my
psyche. What did such an experience mean for the
woman who took part in it? What does it mean,
here depicted, so many centuries later—for me?
for other women? Why, if I read the pictures correctly, is the initiate punished by the stern Erinys
when she kneels to lift the veil from the sacred
phallus? Is she being instructed to seek God under
a more feminine aspect? For the Godhead is surely
neither masculine nor feminine, being beyond our
imagining; but our feeble intuition requires a
metaphor, and for centuries, in our culture, that
metaphor has been masculine.

The initiate of the wall paintings is described as a "self-confident matron," fortyish shall we say? And the goal that she pursues is the goal of middle age. The breakthrough from the unconscious that she has experienced is of the transpersonal nature. Surely (to reiterate) the "mid-life crisis" must be a time of physiological change which has not yet been properly defined. Surely the body must know what the conscious ego has not yet learned to know, that at the mid-point of life the physiological powers have reached their zenith, and all powers, physical and psychological, turn toward and begin already to prepare for death. (In a few women, the mid-point of life seems to coincide with the menopause, but for most not; these appear to be two different phenomena.) It is now that the recognition of the value that transcends death becomes imperative, and generally speaking, it would seem that such recognition becomes possible only now except as a matter of faith. For children and still for young adults, the central value is projected; the parent, the priest, the teacher, the mentor, and of course in our day the analyst, may all at various times and to varying extent be its carriers. In the normal course of events, the mid-life turning point, with its natural withdrawal from the mentor relationship, would seem to offer the first opportunity for a confrontation. The danger is that one may identify with the Self, "set it upon his own brow," in Marie's words. And this is I suppose what happens a great deal in our egotistical society. So long as it is somewhat relative, is tempered with a sense of humor, by a recognition that other people don't take one that seriously, people live out their lives with this attitude, with some discomfort, some clashing with the environment, but without being considered seriously disturbed. "It's nice to be omniscient," says a brilliant friend, triumphantly concluding an argument and congratulating himself on it. It's a joke, of course, but he more than half means it.

There is so much that we need to know about this process. What we greatly need is the recording of many individual cases. What various forms does the "centering process," as Dr. Jung described it, take in various individuals? At what age does it typically conclude? As I have said above, because of my own experience, I have thought of the individuation process as coinciding with the mid-life crisis—several years of struggle for psychic autonomy culminating in an event that subordinates the ego and reveals the transcendent center. But is this typical? From other things that Jung says and from my observation I should think that for many people the fifties are a period of great creativity. When people speak of the individuation process as a life-long sequence, are they speaking of a life-long struggle toward a centering event which has not yet occurred? Or are they speaking of a life-long process in which the centering event has occurred at some point, with a further development beyond that? What did Jung mean when he spoke of a "completed individuation" in his old age?

Levinson thinks that in addition to the mid-life transition, there is probably one more important life crisis, at about the age of eighty. But meanwhile, perhaps after Levinson had done this piece of writing, Erikson published an account of such a crisis (or is it the beginning of such a crisis?) in his discussion of Ingmar Bergman's film *Wild Strawberries*, "Reflections on Dr. Borg's Life Cycle." The protagonist of this film is a distinguished though rather rigid seventy-six-year-old doctor who is, on the day encompassed by the film, being honored for his life's work by the bestowal of an honorary degree. Erikson's essay is compelling enough, but it so happened that shortly before I read the essay a friend of mine, also seventy-six years old, had confided in me a deeply impressive dream which contained nearly all the elements that occur in the film. I will venture to list the most important elements of the old man's experience on that day as Erikson recounts them. (1) In the early morning he awakens from a dream which brings home to him the terror of death. (2) During the drive to the cathedral town where he is to receive his degree, he is compelled, in conversation with his daughter-in-law who accompanies him, and through a series of encounters and fantasies, to relive certain crucial events of his life. (3) He receives the degree, and at the moment of receiving it, experiences a sort of illumination which gives it meaning beyond the dimensions of his personal ego. (4) In some way changed by these events, made simpler and humbler, he has a sort of vision of his parents as he knew them when he was a child. He cannot communicate with them, they are too far away, but they recognize him, and through this vision he in some sense enters into his second childhood.

My friend's dream, which I gratefully quote with her permission, is as follows:

I am with a group of people on a safari. The group has many subgroups and I am affiliated with various family groups (my sister, her husband and children; my nephew, his wife and children, etc.). Our mission has a suprapersonal objective and I am happy to be there. Many of the group are unknown to me.

Since I am too old to take the whole trip, they will drop me off in ———— where I shall stay in my childhood home while they go forward.

When we reach ————, we hear there is some trouble with our bus connection and are advised to start walking, following the bus route so we can pick up the bus if it comes. As we walk, I decide I will not get on the bus at all since I am almost home now. The others can take the bus if it comes.

However, the whole party finally arrives at the old family home which is quite empty. My keys from the distant past do not open the door but I have foreseen that possibility and have designed two new keys to open the two locks on the door. The first key does not function very well and I am worried but the second key opens the door and I am home at last!

The young fry throw me kisses and salutes as they move on. One young man whom I do not know lingers on to speak to me. I had been attracted to him on the trip and he evidently reciprocated. We shake hands and say good-by but I say, "I am invited to come back for the summer and I hope I shall do so. Please come to see me so we can continue our relationship." He nods and moves on with the group.

I stand on the porch of "my home" and watch them

move on. I am alone now but not even Golda Meir[4] can feel as fulfilled as I.

I turn to enter the empty and very silent house and tears of reconciliation flow freely as I tell myself, "I am completely alone now but I have come home."

The initial episode of the film, the confrontation with death, has no counterpart in my friend's dream. Neither does the second component, the review of his life by the old man which is forced on him by circumstances, have a strict parallel in the dream. But my friend is a Jungian analysand to whom the review of her life is no novelty, and in her dream she depicts herself as participating with many others in a journey "toward a suprapersonal goal." The review of their lives by old people is legendary, and sometimes becomes tedious to the young, but it seems to be a most important process. William Butler Yeats, who had much to say on old age, describes it not as "recollection in tranquility" but as recollection with emotion:

> and not a day
> But something is recalled,
> My conscience or my vanity appalled.
> ("Vacillation")

My friend is no ordinary person, and if not as eminent as the old doctor in the film, she has not en-

---

4. My friend's footnote: Golda Meir always reminded me of my mother. A rock of Gibraltar in knowing her own worth, not a women's libber but a supreme individual who was also a wife and mother (sort of incidentally). Laotzu had them in mind when he said, "The way to do is to be!"

tirely lacked for rewards in the society she has
served during a long lifetime. But in her case, the
major recognition, the accolade, comes from the
unconscious. Not even if she had been Golda
Meir, whom she greatly admires, could she feel
more deeply fulfilled. And as she enters her childhood home, she has the promise of a further relation with a young man, potentially one would
think a sort of *psychopompos,* a guide for the
soul, who in some sense parallels the young
daughter-in-law of the Bergman film.

This region of life is almost unexplored. "Now
shall I make my soul," said the aging Yeats, and
indeed in these late years we seem to be making
up a bundle to take with us—a bundle of those
things that we think can pass through customs at
the ultimate border. In this task the young animus
(or the anima in a man's case), the young guide,
must be of great assistance, though I understand
the process very little. Like my friend, I have met
this figure in a dream, but there are aging women
for whom the actual relationship to a young man
seems to have great meaning. At our age death
beckons, holds out an invitation, but we cling to
life, to the people, and even to the places and
things, that we love. In a dream, some four or five
years ago, I was in a courtyard somewhere, and
three men approached me. The middle one held
out toward me a glass of pure, sparkling water. I
knew that it was the water of life, and that it por-
tended the death of the body. But I pushed him
away—put my hand on his chest and pushed him
bodily, crying out, "No! No! Not yet!" And later,

in another dream, I saw a deep and very beautiful green gorge, with a rustic wooden staircase that led down into it. Down this staircase walked in single file a procession of all kinds of people, down into the beautiful depths. They walked on the left side of the stair, each with a hand on the rail. But I was on the opposite side of the stairs, and I was climbing up, not descending, and I was saying to myself, "I can't go down yet; there are still things I have to do."

Meantime in the everyday world life is a prolonged good-bye. Friends fade and disappear. My husband and I, partners now for fifty years, each see our bodily decay mirrored in the other: strength diminishes; coordination, balance, eyesight begin to fail; memory fails. When my ten grandchildren were little, I thought nothing could be more beautiful; but now that they are teenagers and young adults, they are simply dazzling. And the nuclear shadow hangs over them all. God shield them. But the task remains. If I ever get the writing of this essay out of the way, working as I do with diminished energy in time snatched from my day-to-day labors—there is a picture I should like to paint. I should like to paint a vine, starting in the center of the paper, which grows out and proliferates until it covers the page. Impossible, practically, with any degree of satisfaction to the eye or to the psyche. But it should occupy such free time as I have for the rest of my days.

Commentary: Mystical Experience in the Modern World

David J. Hufford

In this essay I shall first discuss mystical experiences in general, particularly in the modern world. Then I shall consider the specific details of Genevieve Foster's vision and connect them with examples from similar and contrasting narratives. Gen and I have referred to her experience as a "mystical vision," and already that places us in a difficult situation. The words *mystical* and *vision* both have problems of meaning. According to the *Oxford English Dictionary* the oldest meaning of *vision* is, "Something which is apparently seen otherwise than by ordinary sight; *esp.* an appearance of a prophetic or mystical character . . . supernaturally presented to the mind." This usage goes back at least to the thirteenth century, and it remains the generally accepted meaning when one speaks of a *mystical* vision. Immediately, then, the use of this term brings with it the concept of the supernatural, one of the most contentious subjects in modern thought. This discussion will therefore require a consideration of the intense debate between secular and supernaturalist viewpoints that has raged in our culture at least since the Enlightenment, and of the place of Jungian thought in this debate. I shall argue that the advantage now enjoyed by the secular position, especially in the academic world, is partly a result of biased scholarship and the success of a particular kind of ideological rhetoric. Such a conclusion does not necessitate the acceptance of the supernatural premise, but it does require those who prefer to maintain a thoroughly secular explanation of mystical phenomena to go back to the drawing board.

In this connection, I do recognize that generations of scholars have agonized over the definition and the usefulness of the term *supernatural.* Schools of thought range from the theologians who use *supernatural* exclusively to refer to God and *preternatural* for persons or forces beyond the physical (e.g., demons or ghosts), to the logical positivists who claim that the word has no cognitive meaning, or the radical cultural relativists who argue that the term is a purely Western category not applicable to other cultures.[1] Here I am

---

1. For a useful summary of the cultural relativist argument see Saler, "Supernatural as a Western Category."

using the word in its popular sense: referring to an order of reality that is different from the world of matter and energy and also different from purely subjective imagination, that at least occasionally interacts with this world, and that is in some ways superior to this world. By implication I take this definition to have cognitive meaning and to be in some ways transculturally applicable as a category of thought. Again, this does not constitute an argument that any particular supernatural belief is correct or even that the supernatural realm "really exists," but rather that the idea of its existence is a widely considered possibility that is accessible to rational discussion. The word *vision* in this supernatural sense, then, stands in contrast to the word *hallucination.*

Whereas a vision is the perception of a supernatural "object," as it were, an hallucination is a false perception that has no real object outside the mind. If a person claims actually to perceive (as opposed to imagining or dreaming) an object that is not physically present, these are the only two words that are readily available in English to describe the event. The choice between them is determined by the speaker's evaluation of the alleged perceiver's correctness or error. That evaluation hinges on whether the speaker believes "the supernatural" to exist. To those who deny its existence *mystical vision* is merely a term used by people who are more or less permanently deceived by hallucinations of a religious sort. To those who accept the reality, or at least the possibility, of the supernatural, visions and hallucinations are two

thoroughly different kinds of events. In the case of
an alleged mystical vision there is no good word
to represent the middle ground. Each word contains a bit of description (and only a bit) plus a
very great load of interpretation, and the interpretations are diametrically opposed to one another.
Whenever we find this situation in language it
suggests that the subject under examination is
loaded with emotional importance, so much importance that one can scarcely bring it up without
simultaneously showing one's colors and indicating a willingness to fight. It is as if *politician* were
to be replaced by the words *cad* and *paragon.* It
would make it a good deal more awkward to discuss elected officials. awkward, but accurate.

Let us now consider what is meant by *mystical.* Turning again to the *OED* we find that its
oldest meaning is, "Having a certain spiritual character or import by virtue of a connexion or union
with God transcending human understanding."
More recent meanings include "occult," and "hidden and obscure." In the development of these two
streams of meaning we may again see the tension
between the naturalist (in the materialist sense)
and the supernaturalist. To the supernaturalist the
mystical experience is so full of meaning that it
can never be fully "unpacked" by human reason
and discourse. To the skeptic the obscurity of
mystical experience is the refuge of the prophet or
priest who really has no answers. Efforts to understand mystical experience generally reflect one of
these two perspectives and clearly illustrate two
opposing orientations toward *mystery*, a word and

a concept closely related to *mystical*. In the modern, secular sense a mystery is a puzzle that has not yet been solved, as in the mystery of quasars or a murder mystery. Such a mystery presents the observer with a set of facts that do not seem to make sense. When the sense is finally extracted the mystery is gone. In the religious usage a mystery is precisely the opposite. It is something that is so full of meaning that human reason can never exhaust it. It is not totally impervious to reason, and mystics and nonmystic religionists alike return repeatedly to mysteries for more and more meaning. This includes both mysteries within creation, such as the meaning of suffering, and those that transcend creation, like the nature of God. There are, of course, some simplistic approaches to the religious explication of such mysteries that attempt to treat them as mysterious only in the puzzle-solving sense. This is the approach that Job's friends took when they explained his suffering as merely the result of a proud refusal to acknowledge his sinfulness and ask forgiveness. The Gnostic search for secret solutions for a select few is a similar response to mystery. People with mystical experience are unlikely to make this error, because they have personally encountered something that they cannot ever fully describe, let alone explain. Yet mystics seem never to tire of returning to the recollection of those experiences to bring back more and more description and interpretation, for what is true of the meaning of mysteries is also true of their description. Mystical experience is not ineffable in the sense that it cannot be described in human language, as has often been suggested, but rather in that the description can never be complete.

Some mystics and students of mysticism argue that there is only one kind of mystical experience and that it is variously described and interpreted; others have devised whole catalogues of types and variants. There is, however, a particular element that all present as the most important. This is the experience of "union." In religious mysticism this is mystical union with God; in nontheistic mysticism it is union with nature or the universe. For those who choose the mystical path as their primary occupation, mystical union is the most perfect thing that can happen in this life.[2] Although mystics all recognize that other kinds of mystical experience can occur and may have validity, they are never considered to be goals of the mystical life and are generally regarded with suspicion.

The experience of mystical union was the prototype for a survey of mystical experiences of Americans carried out by Andrew Greeley at the National Opinion Research Center (NORC) and published in 1975 as *The Sociology of the Paranormal: A*

---

2. In reading through my essay, Gen has pointed out that there are problems with this modern use of the term *union,* and I agree with her although I have not been able to find a solution. The word is used in an extremely varied way in the literature of mysticism, and as suggested by my use often refers to an "experience." However, in classic mystical language this should refer more to a way of life than a transitory experience. Let it be understood, then, that for convenience I am using the term in its most common sense. For a description of its more technical and correct sense see references to the "Unitive Life" in, for example, Underhill, *Mysticism.*

Reconnaisance. Greeley's survey asked about three distinct forms of "paranormal" experiences: (1) déjà vu, extrasensory perception, and clairvoyance; (2) "contact with the dead;" and (3) mystical experience. The project was carried out in 1973 with approximately 1,460 respondents chosen in an NORC national sample. The survey's "mysticism question" was constructed by Greeley after a thorough review of mystical literature for descriptions of the experience of union. The wording that he used was, "Have you ever felt as though you were very close to a powerful spiritual force that seemed to lift you out of yourself?" He received startlingly high rates of positive response to this and his other two questions. For mystical experience 35 percent of the sample responded positively and 61 percent negatively (3 percent could not answer the question). The positive response category consisted of 18 percent (of the total sample) who reported one or two mystical experiences, 12 percent who reported several, and 5 percent who said that they had them "often." Because this is such a high rate of positive response it is important to keep in mind that these people were responding specifically to a question derived from classic descriptions of mystical experience. They were not simply responding on the basis of whatever they might have considered to be mystical in a popular sense. In fact, the word mystical was not used in the questionnaire.

Greeley found that all age groups from teenagers through those in their seventies were well represented among his mystics. Positive responses

were most common among those in their fifties
(43 percent), but no age group provided fewer than
30 percent positive answers (teenagers were lowest
with 32 percent positive responses). Both the overall frequency and the age distribution of these answers are quite different from what the modern
stereotype of mystical experience would lead one
to expect. Greeley collected a great deal of data
about his respondents, and his monograph involves a very extensive analysis of that information. Of greatest interest to us at present is the
fact that his findings, in general, ran counter to
stereotypical expectations, expectations that reflect the modern hostility to such experiences. Although intense emotions were frequently described,
these experiences were reported as having been
fundamentally cognitive; that is, they involved
knowing something, although that knowledge was
very difficult to express fully. This is a characteristic of mystical experience that has often been
overlooked by recent analysts who concentrate on
mystical events as feeling states. Nonetheless,
mystics have always asserted that their experiences brought them knowledge. This is what William James referred to as the "noetic" quality of
mystical experience in his monumental work, *The
Varieties of Religious Experience* (1902). Whether
the nonmystic understands that knowledge or considers it valid is beside the point. Failure to take
this feature into account makes it very easy to
confuse the mystical experience, as a distinct
state, with a great variety of other experiences
that are characterized by intense feelings and

often metaphorically described by words borrowed from mysticism such as *ecstasy* and *rapture.*

Perhaps the most important manner in which Greeley's findings deviated from the conventional academic view of mystical experience is that his mystics tended to be college-educated, with middle-class incomes, and in a "state of psychological well-being substantially higher than the national average" (p. 62) as measured by the Bradburn psychological well-being scale (see *The Structure of Psychological Well-Being).* The conventional notion that mystical experience is a neurotic escape common to unhappy and maladjusted people is certainly not supported by these findings.

Greeley performed a variety of analyses to discover which of the frequently reported features of the mystical experience were most strongly connected with the strikingly good psychological state suggested by the Bradburn scale. He found first of all that a set of features clearly resembling classic mystical descriptions—"passivity . . . ineffability . . . a new sense of life [and] the experience of being bathed in light" (p. 77)—showed a very high correlation with psychological well-being. The more "authentic" the experience in classic mystical terms, then, the more likely the person reporting it to show a "positive affect balance." Greeley also found that those whose descriptions fit this classic model had very high levels of confidence in the survival of the human person after death. In fact, further analysis of the survey data showed belief in personal survival of physical death to be the single factor most strongly connected with psychological well-being. While this connection of mystical experience with supernatural belief is not surprising, it does clearly support the interpretation that Greeley's overall findings involve the religious mystical experience *per se*, and not some other state that his respondents mistakenly connected with his question.

Greeley's study did not elicit detailed phenomenological descriptions of the experiences involved, relying instead on a checklist of possible features to obtain comparable descriptors. Also, although the question is well conceived and Greeley's subsequent analyses suggest that the bulk of his respondents understood his intent, the question does have elements that are open to more than one interpretation. Feeling "close to a powerful spiritual force" and feeling "lifted out of yourself" can both be understood metaphorically as well as literally. For this reason I undertook, in collaboration with Donald Rumbaugh, a student at Penn State College of Medicine, a small study to determine how often a positive response to Greeley's mysticism question might refer to something other than mystical experience as traditionally understood. The sample for our project consisted of thirty randomly selected hospital patients with a variety of diagnoses, with psychiatric cases specifically excluded. Although the number of subjects was too small for us to draw statistical conclusions with confidence, the results were interesting. We asked each person Greeley's mysticism question and then tape-recorded a complete description of the experience or experiences to which each positive response referred.

Of our thirty subjects, fourteen responded positively to the question, thirteen negatively and three could not answer. By analyzing the descriptions of our respondents' experiences, the positive responses were divided into false positives and genuine positives according to the manner in which Greeley's question was interpreted and the similarity of the descriptions to those given in the literature of mysticism. In this way we concluded that there were eight false positive responses: one respondent had interpreted the "lifting out of self" as implying a general loss of control and described no "spiritual force" at all; another took the "lifting out" to simply mean feeling "uplifted" in general, and also failed to describe any spiritual force; six other respondents also took "lifting out" to simply mean feeling "uplifted" in the metaphorical sense, and interpreted "closeness to a powerful spiritual force" to refer to their religious belief that God (a powerful spiritual force) is always close.

The six descriptions that we classified as indicating genuine positive responses included unusual sensations associated with the feeling of being "lifted out" and were very specific about the presence of a "powerful spiritual force." Four of the six described feeling that they actually had left their physical bodies. Of these four, two respondents described what are currently known as "near death experiences," to which we shall turn our attention shortly.

Despite the small sample size, then, our findings supported those reported by Greeley. Although a substantial number of positive responses to the question as worded do not refer to what is usually indicated by the term "mystical experience," almost half do. Furthermore, the number of those that do is a strikingly large percentage (20 percent) of the total population surveyed. Also, we found no connection between positive responses in our sample and any record of psychological problems, based on the medical histories and hospital charts of our subjects.

II

The conventional negative reaction to mysticism has focused primarily on efforts at reduction; that is, efforts to explain that it is something less than it seems and that the claims of its adherents are naive misunderstandings. And whether one agrees with this set of "explanations" or not, they are important to understand, because they comprise the dominant intellectual response to mysticism in modern times.

The oldest form of this reduction is the equation of mystical experience with mental illness. In the Bible, for instance, we are told that on Pentecost the Apostles "began to speak in foreign languages as the Spirit gave them the gift of speech. . . . Many of those listening heard them speaking in their native languages and were amazed, while others 'laughed it off.' 'They have been drinking too much new wine,' they said" (Jerusalem Bible, Acts 2:1–13). This passage has been variously interpreted as referring to xenoglossy or glossolalia on the part of the Apostles and the gift of knowledge on the part of those listeners who understood them. All of these charismatic gifts fit the description of mystical experience in general and are connected with a form of mystical union. The skeptic's response at the time was to attribute the episode to one of the most universally known abnormal psychological states, alcoholic intoxication.

As popular as this deprecating explanation of mystical experiences has been over the centuries, it truly came into its own with the development of modern psychological theory. In 1911 Evelyn Underhill summed up the psychological approach very succinctly, together with her own unwillingness to accept it: "Yet it may well be doubted whether that flame of living love which could, for one dazzling instant, weld body and soul in one, was really a point of weakness in a saint: whether . . . the powers of St. Paul and St. Teresa are fully explained on a basis of epilepsy or hysteria; whether . . . it is as scientific as it looks to lump together all visions and voices—from Wandering Willy to the Apocalypse of St. John—as examples of unhealthy cerebral activity" (*Mysticism,* p. 267).

Sixty-five years later the Committee on Psychiatry and Religion of the Group for the Advancement of Psychiatry (GAP) published *Mysticism: Spiritual Quest or Psychic Disorder?* summing up recent thought on the equation of mystical experience with mental illness. In a chapter entitled "The Psychological Point of View" characterizing the experience of mystical union as a trance state, the committee offers the following summary:

Both the ego state of the trance experience and its content strongly suggest that it is a regression to an infantile condition. The content of the trance fantasy symbolizes the gratification of desires to see the parent or parents, [*sic*] especially hidden or wondrous aspects; desires to approach, enter into, or experience some physical contact with the parent; or desires to unite or become one with the parent. . . .

[In] conclusion: Confronted with an unacceptable reality—intrapsychic, personal or social—the subject turns his back on that reality, excluding it from his consciousness and psychically destroying it. He replaces it with a new inner reality which he has so designed that it gratifies rather than frustrates him. This process represents a rebirth, a return to a state of mind characteristic of his infancy, when he was able to deal with frustration and disappointment by retreating to a world of fantasy and when he also enjoyed a firm and intimate union with his parents. Achieving this union once again in fantasy, he now feels vigorous and powerful, no longer dependent upon the whims of other people. (P. 781)

In this chapter the committee specifically underlines what it considers the important connections between mystical experience and three abnormal states: hallucinogenic intoxication, schizophrenia, and seizures. The visions of mysticism are said to result from the withdrawal of attention from the external world to the world of internal sensations with "the sense of reality . . . transferred from the outside inward with the permission of an indulgent ego which . . . foregoes strict reality testing" (p. 778). This inwardly focused state is called "infantile" because it is one which people usually outgrow as their perceptual capacities mature (p. 780). The distinction between the psychotic and the mystic is made on the basis of whether this abnormal state is obligatory and cannot be reversed by an act of will (psychotic) or can be "voluntarily intensified or resisted or terminated" (mystic) (p. 780). But the committee goes on to note that this distinction is not always clear-cut and that in some cases it is very difficult to determine whether the subject is a mystic or a psychotic. Mysticism is seen, then, as being a psychological defense that is immature and that misrepresents reality (part of the definition of a defense mechanism), but that under some circumstances may serve a useful function. These circumstances range from ordinary life events in the very weak to overwhelming environmental stress in the normal individual. In all cases, though, it is a departure from normal, healthy, and mature ways of coping with life.

To give an idea of the extent to which this model can be applied to specific mystical experiences and visions I shall quote one example from the epilogue to the book: "Saint Catherine of Siena was a mystic who reported having highly developed feelings of awe at the age of five, when she saw the Lord 'in the most sacred and awe-inspiring garb imaginable' above the Sienese Church of San Domenico. Greenacre has suggested that childhood feelings of awe which may later be associated with inspiration, creativity and religious feeling are often derived from awe (as distinguished from envy) of the phallus. In the girl, awe is more liable to be aroused . . . if the child sees an adult phallus rather than a boy's" (p. 816).

One consequence of our growing awareness of the frequent occurrence of mystical experience among ordinary people must be to complicate the interpretation of the basic criteria for differentiating between mysticism and psychosis. The distinction noted just above, the alleged voluntariness of the mystic's experience, does not stand up well when examined in connection with the spontaneous mystical experiences of ordinary people, and Gen's vision is a good case in point. She did not bring on the experience voluntarily, she did not voluntarily modify it during the five days that it persisted, she tried but was unable to prevent it from ending, and her repeated efforts to recapture the experience were unsuccessful. Even career mystics would generally deny voluntary control over their experiences, beyond the development of receptivity, since they have consistently stressed that theirs is a passive role in what happens. Most books on the mystical life, particularly those of a religious nature, emphasize that the most perfect forms of mystical experience are in no sense *caused* by the individual. The mystic's role is generally described as being an active one only at the beginning of the mystical path, and then only in the cultivation of such religious virtues as charity and humility, and in such practices as meditation and verbal prayer. These are said to prepare the mystic for *infused contemplation* which is given to the mystic by God and requires quiet submission. In fact, if this experience jolts the mystic into mental activity, this activity itself will terminate the experience. Furthermore, the development of receptivity does not guarantee a certain quantity of infused contemplation, nor does it give the mystic the ability to turn it on and off.[3] The skeptic can argue over the exact nature of the mystic's conscious and unconscious part in this, but the process in all of the great mystical traditions is certainly not voluntary in the sense that psychedelic experience is voluntary in the person who intentionally takes an hallucinogen. In ordinary people even the intentional cultivation of receptivity is absent.

The implications of the mystical experiences of modern, ordinary people are even more important for the issue of belief and psychopathology. It has long been recognized that normal people occasionally experience hallucinations, although presumably less often than do psychotics. The difference is generally held to be that the normal person recognizes the hallucination as such while the psychotic believes it to be "real." The most frequently recognized exception to this difference has involved membership in a group that provides consensual validation of a particular kind of hallucination or "false belief" (e.g., a contemplative religious community). This point is summed up in another

---

3. For an excellent discussion of this point in terms that are fully within one of the great mystical traditions, in this case the Roman Catholic, see Thomas Merton, *The Ascent to Truth,* particularly chap. 14, "Intelligence in the Prayer of Quiet." On the impossibility of voluntary acquisition of infused contemplation (obviously a contradiction in terms) Merton quotes from St. Teresa of Avila: "What a strange kind of belief it is that when God has willed that a toad should fly, He should wait for it to do so by its own efforts" (p. 220).

book published by GAP entitled *The Psychic Function of Religion in Mental Illness and Health* (1968). Speaking again of "religious fantasies" the committee states that: "religion often demands belief in things that cannot be verified by direct observation or by logical inference from observable data. . . . However, what the schizophrenic chooses to ignore is the fact that the credibility of ideas is normally established either by reality-testing or by the sanction of the community; it is community sanction that exempts religious beliefs from the ordinary requirements of reality-testing. Yet the schizophrenic lacks *both* reality-testing and community sanction" (p. 680).

This distinction holds true for schizophrenics, and it may appear also to hold in the case of mystics who live in mystical communities and, therefore, have community sanction. However, a whole host of ordinary people who are not schizophrenics may now be seen to come down on the wrong side of this distinction. Better than a quarter of the population of the United States now appears to have had one or more mystical experiences that they believed at the time—*and afterward*—to be real in spite of a lack of positive community sanction; in fact, in spite of strong and well-known negative community sanctions. Aware of these negative sanctions, Genevieve Foster told only four people of her vision until more than thirty years had passed. Greeley found that almost none of his "mystics" had ever told anyone of their experience, nor had the subjects that Rumbaugh and I interviewed. The same is true of a variety of

other "numinous experiences" that have recently
been found to be common in the general population. If these people are not all undiagnosed
schizophrenics, or people who have experienced
brief and self-limited psychotic episodes in the
midst of ordinary life—and there is every reason
to resist such an interpretation—how can we account for the failure of this criterion to distinguish them from psychotics? I am quite certain
that the explanation lies in the fundamental difference between psychotic experience and mystical
experience. We are not, in actuality, faced with
the need to distinguish between normal and abnormal responses to an abnormal experience. Instead we are faced with the need to distinguish between abnormal experiences and experiences that
are not merely normal but that may well indicate
substantially superior psychological health.

When we consider this aspect of our subject,
the enormously strong and effective barriers to
honest communication about such experiences,
we come to a truly novel answer for one of the
most persistent questions that scholars of belief
have asked during this century: Why does belief in
an external, nonmaterial reality persist in the face
of widespread education, modernization, and so
forth, which are implicitly hostile to such beliefs?
It has long been accepted by most who have considered this question that mystical experiences of
all sorts and the beliefs that accompany them are
largely shaped and encouraged by tradition (positive community sanctions) except in the case of
psychotics; that as such (unrealistic, infantile) tra-

ditions encounter more modern and effective means of dealing with genuine reality they will less and less encourage such experiences; and that in consequence the experiences themselves will become less common except among psychotics. That expectation gained a great deal of support as Western religion became less and less mystical in the late nineteenth and early twentieth centuries. At the same time fewer and fewer people in the mainstream of Western culture spoke of mystical experience. This was, of course, interpreted as evidence of the expected decline of such "defensive behaviors" among the sophisticated. In fact, this expectation seemed to have been so well demonstrated by the 1960s that there has been widespread shock and alarm in response to what has been variously called the occult revival, a retreat from rationality, or a spiritual renewal, that has been increasingly evident since the late sixties. Conventional explanations have included "future shock," a reaction against an excessively technological society, fear of nuclear holocaust, and insufficient science education in the public schools.

The answer that I am suggesting is that the traditions accompanying mystical experiences in the past were more derived from those experiences than vice versa; that is, mystical theology, mystical communities, and folk belief about an order of reality beyond the physical have been the result of persistent, universal, human experiences that even today do not yield to any simple explanation. The apparent fulfillment of modern expectations about such experiences and attendant beliefs has been the result of religious *institutions* yielding to powerful, "official," social pressures, leaving ordinary people with less and less opportunity to discuss openly their nonordinary experiences. They have not, apparently, had fewer of them, and they have not been less impressed by them. They have simply been a lot more quiet about them. No matter how many times I consider this situation, and the developments of the past fifteen years or so, I have never been able to think of a better analogy than the folktale of The Emperor's New Clothes. As long as every individual believes that only he can see that the emperor is really naked, no one will mention that embarrassing fact for fear of appearing a fool. But as soon as one or two brave souls begin to describe the reality that they perceive, one is faced with a tidal wave of "disillusionment" in the technical sense. The main difference is that not everyone has had a mystical experience, so many people must base their personal decision about "what is really going on" on a reasoned consideration of the testimony of others. As the quantity and quality of that testimony increases, the conclusions of the ordinary nonmystic are modified, as if most citizens listened to radio accounts of the emperor parading in his new clothes and had to infer the cause of the increasing commotion and decide between official pronouncements and unofficial eyewitness accounts.

If this is approximately what has been happening to mystical experience in our culture, then the psychopathological "explanation" has been primarily a mechanism of social control. It has been a means for providing the strongest kind of devaluation of mystical experience. It has not only set up rules about the manner in which the subject could be discussed, but has provided a means of enforcement through the elaboration of diagnostic criteria that place the honest but isolated mystic in the same category as the psychotic. But let us be very clear on this point. I am *not* suggesting that schizophrenia is simply what an unappreciative modernity calls mystical experience. (One obvious difference is that schizophrenics are either less concerned about how others will respond to their experiences and beliefs—or less able to predict those responses—and are therefore much less discreet about them than mystics are.) Some enthusiastic supporters of mysticism have suggested that all schizophrenics are really mystics and prophets, to the detriment of both genuine schizophrenics and the better understanding of mysticism. Schizophrenia undoubtedly does exist, and undoubtedly many schizophrenics have religious delusions and hallucinations just as many of them have political, technological, and sexual delusions and hallucinations. The point is that schizophrenia is different from genuine mysticism to as great a degree as genuine politics, technology, and healthy sexuality are different from schizophrenia. It is not stretching the point, in fact, to compare the effects of the equation of mysticism with psychosis in modern culture to the equation of political dissent with psychosis in the Soviet Union. While the "mystical problem" has not and could not be as vigorously prosecuted in the West as the "dissident problem" has been in Russia, the damping effect on open discourse has been similar.

An additional effect of this situation has been to purge most of our religious institutions of their mystical traditions so thoroughly that it is now very difficult for them to respond to the growing demand for an articulate framework for the expression, evaluation, and incorporation of mystical experience. This is a dangerous situation because, according to mystical tradition, these experiences can be as hazardous as they can be helpful, and it is skilled guidance that makes the difference.

III

Psychopathology has not been the only route taken to the reduction of mystical experience. At the turn of the century there were scholars who recognized a link between mystical experience and creativity, but who were quite hostile to the traditional religious framework within which they found those experiences discussed. From this ambivalence developed an approach that regarded mystical experience as not *less* than its adherents have claimed, but rather *more.* (Of course, what constitutes "more" and what "less" depends on one's viewpoint.) This perspective has held that all genuine mystical experiences arise from a single natural state and that they can be a wonderfully fruitful resource for human development. The apparent differences, and the fact that some mystical experiences seem to have been associated with disastrous personal and social consequences, are attributed to the various methods that have developed for interpreting, and at the same time shaping, those experiences. This approach views the alleged experiential bases of all religions as referring to this one natural state. This has most often involved discussion of Christian mysticism and Eastern, particularly Buddhist, mysticism. It is suggested that local variations are the result of institutionalization and attendant political processes, naive folk belief, and general cultural difference. In contrast, the mystics of different religious traditions, when they have been aware of the existence of other mystical traditions, have generally been interested in the similarities with their own but have stopped well short of considering them identical. From the all-mystical-experience-is-one perspective this is seen as an understandable but backward response, occasioned by the conservatism and inertia that characterize religious systems.

The other major element in this approach, which for convenience I shall call the Perennial Philosophy (the term used by Aldous Huxley in *The Doors of Perception*), is the assertion that religious mysticism of all kinds is also identical in essence to what is often called "nature mysticism." The nature mystic is one whose experience of union is with nature, with the material universe, rather than with a supernatural being or order that transcends nature. An excellent example of such an experience is given by R. C. Zaehner in his book *Mysticism: Sacred and Profane.* He quotes the Irish novelist, Forrest Reid:

It was as if I had never realized before how lovely the world was. I lay down on my back in the warm, dry

moss and listened to the skylark singing as it mounted
up from the fields near the sea into the dark clear sky.
No other music ever gave me the same pleasure as that
passionately joyous singing. It was a kind of leaping,
exultant ecstasy, a bright, flame-like sound, rejoicing in
itself. And then a curious experience befell me. It was
as if everything that had seemed to be external and
around me were suddenly within me. The whole world
seemed to be within me. It was within me that the
trees waved their green branches, it was within me that
the skylark was singing, it was within me that the hot
sun shone, and that the shade was cool. A cloud rose in
the sky, and passed in a light shower that pattered on
the leaves, and I felt its freshness dropping into my
soul, and I felt in all my being the delicious fragrance
of the earth and the grass and the plants and the rich
brown soil. I could have sobbed with joy. (Pp. 40–41)

Nature mystics frequently state that these experiences transcend space and time, and it can easily be seen from this example that they can involve a very intense kind of union. These are
things that they have in common with religious
mysticism. Another point of similarity is that nature mystics often say that their experience has
given them a realization of the "irrelevance" of
death. In other words, nature mystics, like religious mystics, report that their experiences yield
an attitude toward death that is different from the
one that seems to come most easily to the nonmystic: that is, that death is a very important fact
and rather to be feared. There is, nonetheless, an
important difference between a belief in personal
survival (religious mysticism) and a conviction
that death does not matter (nature mysticism).

The former may well generate the latter, but the reverse is not necessarily true. Of course, exponents of the Perennial Philosophy approach consider the idea of personal survival as a crude, "literal-minded" version of the perception of the irrelevance of death.[4]

Among the major recent proponents of this approach was Abraham Maslow, a prime mover in the development of "humanistic psychology," also called the Third Force Movement in psychology because it presented itself as an alternative to behaviorism and psychoanalysis, although it has rather a lot in common with the latter. Humanistic psychology is directly associated with the modern humanistic movement in general—that is, humanism as opposed to theism. Put simply it is a reaction against the pathology orientation of psychoanalysis and the absence of concern with "higher values" in the rest of psychology in general; it also opposes the tendency for human value systems to be rooted in systems of supernatural belief—"religious", as that term has been traditionally understood, although some humanists, Maslow included, have sought to redefine religion in a way that includes naturalistic systems of belief. Thus it is not surprising that when humanistic psychology has concerned itself with the mystical experience it has found nature mysticism more congenial than theistic or religious mysticism.

---

4. See, for example, Alex Comfort's article from the Perennial Philosophy perspective, "On Going to the Forest: Geriatrics and Pastoral Thanatology."

Maslow's book *Religions, Values and Peak Experiences* is a vigorous and influential presentation of this point of view. He considers the religious systems of the world to have been commendable attempts at producing human fulfillment and sound systems of values; he sees them as derived primarily from mystical—or in his terminology, "peak"—experiences; and he sees them as having failed to achieve true success because of prescientific superstitious belief in the supernatural, and because of subversion by the literal mindedness and conservatism of "legalistic-ecclesiastic . . . organization men" (p. 21). Maslow wanted to purify mysticism and religion in general of what he saw as theistic superstition. He urged that the world's religions should agree to teach that which they all share, namely that which is common to all peak experiences.

> This something common, this something which is left over after we peel away all the localisms, all the accidents of particular languages or particular philosophies, all ethnocentric phrasings, all those elements which are *not* common, we may call the "core-religious experience" or the "transcendent experience." (P. 20)

What is it that Maslow sees as *not* common in all of this? "Only, it seems, the concept of supernatural beings or of supernatural laws or forces; and I must confess my feeling that . . . this difference doesn't seem to be of any great consequence" (p. 55). He calls these supernatural details "ethnocentric phrasings of peak-experiences" and asserts that:

All these experiences are described in about the same general way; the language and the concrete contents may be different, indeed must be different. These experiences are essentially ineffable . . . which is also to say that they are unstructured (like Rorschach ink-blots). Small wonder it is then that the mystic, trying to describe his experience, can do it only in a local, culture-bound, ignorance-bound, language-bound way, confusing his description of the experience with whatever explanation of it and phrasing of it is most readily available to him in his time and place. (P. 72)

He then closes his one-and-a-half-page section on ethnocentric phrasings with the following comment: "I have, therefore, paid no attention to these localisms since they cancel one another out" (p. 73).

A more recent and no less forceful statement along the same lines has been made by Alex Comfort. In his archly titled book *I and That: Notes on the Biology of Religion,* Comfort says of mystics that "in a culture with few strong religious sentiments they may not see their experiences as 'religious' even if they cultivate them. . . . in religiocentric cultures they make the religious noises appropriate to the culture, and incorporate their visionary activities with them, as did St. Teresa and Ramakrishna" (p. 36). In an article about the value of the nontheistic mystical experience for the aged ("On Going to the Forest"), Comfort becomes quite specific on two points that are particularly characteristic of this perspective. He calls beliefs in personal survival of physical death "denial mythologies" and insists that they are not a natural and integral part of "oceanic experience," as he calls nontheistic mystical experience.[5] He then shows the preference that adherents of this approach to mysticism have for Eastern religions: "The reason that Buddhism and Hinduism have dealt more effectively with the issue of life-cycle, death, and vision than much conventional Christianity is that, popular belief in 'heaven' or 'reincarnation' apart, their chief religious resource has been personal oceanic experience in which . . . the basic relief of anxieties over cessation and not-being comes from a personal experience of the irrelevance of such anxieties to the actual form of reality" (p. 35). Selective reading of Eastern religious literature and sacred texts, together with a careful exclusion of major elements of Buddhism and Hinduism as actually practiced in their home settings, has become a popular way for Westerners to assert the support of an ancient tradition for a nonsupernatural religion, including a nonsupernatural mysticism. On this score, Comfort is at

---

5. Freud coined the term *oceanic experience* to describe feelings of oneness with the universe in his book *Civilization and Its Discontents* (1930). He tentatively identified this feeling—extending from very general to very specific varieties—as a source of religious energy not necessarily connected with the particular "illusions" of religious systems (p. 1). He suggested that its origin was to be found in the infantile state prior to the recognition of boundaries between the self and the external environment, with regression to that state being an "attempt at religious consolation" in the face of harsh reality. This has remained a dominant psychoanalytic theme in theories concerning mysticism; in 1968, for example, *The Encyclopedia of Psychoanalysis* identified the oceanic feeling as "the source of all religious feeling . . . of the religious spirit," citing Freud on the difference between this and the desire of the normal individual for "growth to maturity" (p. 280).

least forthright in granting that one must discount quite a lot of these religions as actually believed and practiced in order to achieve a fully sanitized and secular version. Maslow and Comfort are useful examplars of this perspective and show the current tendency for it to include both psychodynamic and psychobiological theorists.

IV

No doubt I have already made it clear that I take strong exception to the conclusions of this camp; as strong as the exception that I take to those who reduce the mystical to psychopathology. First of all, this view makes it a criticism that mystics of the past, and the mystical systems of which many of them were a part, were "culture-bound." This is a condition that Maslow, a rather antitraditional writer, actually equated with "ignorance-bound" in the passage quoted above. The implication is that Western thought, having finally reached the point which culminates in the particular author's point of view, has transcended culture. There is a triumphant sense of having finally arrived at objective knowledge. The mysteries are all about to be explained—never mind that the new breakthrough is a reaction to the errors of an earlier approach that only a few decades ago had itself appeared to arrive finally at the objective knowledge that had eluded *its* predecessor. I don't mean to suggest that there is never any genuine intellectual progress. But if the lessons of the past are any indication, there is generally far less finality at any given moment than the scholars of that moment believe. One reason for this is that all scholarship is culturally conditioned, as is the rest of human behavior. Even the investigations of the physical sciences have been shown to be heavily influenced by social, cultural, and psychological factors. The effects of these factors on students of human behavior, of course, are even greater, just as their subject matter is more complex, elusive, and personally important to the investigator. The tendency of the academic community to deny the obvious fact that its enterprise is embedded in culture has hinged on the notion that scholars are personally disinterested, pursuing truth for truth's sake. Certainly such a state is a splendid ideal, but anyone familiar with the system of values and rewards within which the professional thinker works and lives must have some reservations as to whether this ideal is ever really achieved. The essence of good scholarship is the recognition of personal bias and the careful attempt to control for it. Most of the proponents of the Perennial Philosophy appear to have scant appreciation of the programmatic and ideological dimensions of their "findings." They discard those elements of traditional belief that they do not share and take as fundamental those that they do find congenial. More than anything else they appear to be, to use Maslow's words, the "organization men" of new, secular religions.

Secular is the key word here, and the effort to discredit supernatural beliefs and to discard any experience that would appear to support such beliefs emerges as the most important goal. As shown by Maslow and Comfort, this is done by explaining the beliefs as cultural mechanisms for psychological defenses (e.g., the denial of death) and for social control (e.g., divine right of kings, "pie in the sky" for oppressed peasants, fear of hell to reinforce legal sanctions). The beliefs are then said to produce the contents of those experiences that appear to support them: those who believe in God imagine that they are merging with God when they are in fact merely experiencing a wholly salutary awareness of their continuity with the rest of physical creation. Or the experience is actually the same as the nature mystic's but is described in different terms. For example, the word *God* is used in place of the word *universe* because of the traditional association of religious language with such experiences. It is suggested that both kinds of effect interact and constitute the local, cultural bias. The features of experiences that do not suggest the supernatural are accepted as constituting "reality as we now know it" — the human nervous system, the external physical universe, and some sort of heightened and adaptive interaction between the two.

This effort to explain away those mystical experiences that are inherently supernaturalistic is part of a set of academic ideas that have a long history in the study of belief in general. This set of ideas has developed as an increasingly secular academic community has sought to explain why, in all cultures, experiences are alleged that appear to support a belief in a supernatural order of existence, complete with supernatural persons. Where there is a vigorous tradition of supernatural belief, a variety of past and present experiences are said to have given rise to and have helped to maintain the traditional beliefs. ("We hold this belief because these events took place.") The academic response has been to assert that the link is real but the causal connection is just the reverse. That is, it is the set of beliefs (explained by a variety of psychological, social, and cultural theories) that has given rise to and helped to maintain the experiences. ("Those events took place—or seemed to take place—because you hold that belief.") I call this conventional academic explanation the *cultural source hypothesis.* It is plausible and is useful for the examination of all sorts of supernatural beliefs and the academic responses to them. Elsewhere I have used this concept to examine the beliefs about supernatural assault that are found in all cultures within a variety of interpretive frameworks ranging from witchcraft to vampirism.[6] The associated terrifying experiences are mystical in the sense of being interpreted as "spiritual" although evil—a universally recognized aspect of spirituality. The difference in reported contents between these experiences and the classes of mystical experience that we have been considering makes them particularly useful for comparison.

These terrifying experiences are what was originally meant by the word *nightmare* before that term came to mean a bad dream. In modern Western culture the experience involved corre-

---

6. See *The Terror That Comes in the Night.*

sponds to the medical category of sleep paralysis, but is only partially explained by current knowledge of that state. I have been able to demonstrate that the contents of this terrifying experience, when gathered with careful attention to detail and to local variations in language, constitute a pattern that transcends culture and that conforms very well to the various supernatural belief traditions of which it forms a part. The actual details of the experience do not vary according to the victim's background, prior beliefs, or knowledge of a cultural model for the experience. Furthermore, over half of those experiences occurring in the absence of a cultural model include all the details that the cultural source hypothesis attempts to explain by cultural shaping. Therefore, the cultural source hypothesis in its present form is inadequate to explain why the experience is not only common in other cultures, but has been experienced by at least 15 percent of modern North Americans. In fact, the causal connection between these bizarre experiences and related traditions appears to be analogous to that which I have suggested between mystical experience and mystical traditions: traditions of supernatural assault found all over the world are the result of a universal human experience that has an inherently supernatural appearance wherever it is found. This by no means proves that these experiences actually are supernatural, but it does indicate that a material explanation of them must proceed in a manner that is considerably different from and more sophisticated than the cultural source hypothesis.

Commentary

A brief example will serve to illustrate the kind of detail that is involved. The following passage is from an interview that I conducted with a medical student concerning an experience he had had as an undergraduate. He had no previous knowledge of, or belief in, such things, and prior to the interview he knew of no one else who had ever experienced an attack. Despite all of the features of his background and his current situation he could not shake the feeling that what had happened to him was objectively real.

What woke me up was the door slamming. "Ok," I thought, "It's my roommate. . . ." I was laying on my back just kinda looking up. And the door slammed and I kinda opened my eyes. I was awake. Everything was light in the room. My roommate wasn't there and the door was still closed. . . .

But the next thing I knew, I realized that I couldn't move. . . . I kind of like gazed over to the door and there was no one there. But the next thing I knew, from one of the areas of the room this grayish, brownish murky presence was there. And it kind of swept down over the bed and I was terrified! . . . It was like nothing I had ever seen before. And I felt—I felt this pressing down all over me. I couldn't breathe. I couldn't move. And the whole thing was that—there was like—I could hear the stereo in the room next to me. I was wide awake, you know. It was a fraternity house. I could hear everything going on all over the house. It was a pretty noisy place. And I couldn't move and I was helpless and I was really—I was really scared. . . . And this murky presence—just kind of—this was *evil!* This was evil! You know, this is weird! You must think I'm a. . . . This thing was *there!* I felt a pressure on me and it was like enveloping me. It was a very, very, very strange thing. And as I remember I struggled. I struggled to move and get out. And—you know, eventually, I think eventually what happened was I kind of like moved my arm. And again the whole thing—just kind of dissipated away. The presence, everything. But everything else just remained the same. The same stereo was playing next door. The same stuff was going on. (*The Terror*, pp. 58–59)

In addition to this class of terrifying experiences there is currently a mounting body of evidence that several other classes of supernatural-appearing experiences are not simply produced by belief, cultural models, and a variety of psychological mechanisms. The "near death experience," of which I shall have more to say in a moment, now seems independent of prior belief and the presence of cultural models. The experience that our culture often terms "seeing a ghost" is also undergoing reexamination in terms of prior belief, distribution in the population, and relationship to psychopathology.[7] So the questions that I am raising about the interrelationship of "mystical experience," culture, belief, and language must be seen against the background of increasing evidence of the inadequacy of academic explanations of super-

---

7. Greeley's "contact with the dead" question (see *The Sociology of the Paranormal*) provided a major contribution to this reexamination. See also, for example, Michael F. Hoyt, "Clinical Notes Regarding the Experience of 'Presences' in Mourning"; W. Dewi Rees, "The Hallucinations of Widowhood"; William Foster Matchett, "Repeated Hallucinatory Experiences as a Part of the Mourning Process Among Hopi Indian Women"; W. Scott MacDonald and Chester W. Oden, Jr., "*Aumakua:* Behavioral Direction Visions in Hawaiians."

natural belief in general. Now I shall turn to some
of the ways that this experience-culture issue has
been examined for mystical experience, and how
such an examination can elucidate the connections between mystical experience *per se* and
other forms of "supernatural experience."

V

One approach has been the comparison of
printed accounts of mystical experience. Depending on the scholar's intent these comparisons may
be used either to highlight differences among various classes of experience or to show their similarities. These comparisons often use fairly complete
descriptions of the experiences involved. Surveys
such as Greeley's are more systematic, using a variety of methods to elicit information about the
occurrence, effects, distribution, and so forth, of
the experiences. These surveys rarely include complete descriptions in the words of the subject,
more often relying on yes or no responses to questions whose construction is intended to identify
either specific kinds of experience or specific
kinds of respondents. The two approaches are
complementary, each having its own strengths
and weaknesses. They are closely related in that
the set of experiences to which one's conclusions
apply will be determined by the criteria with
which one starts: in the one case these are the criteria for deciding which of the many descriptions
of intense experience available in biographies, case
histories, journals, interview studies, and so forth
will be considered for comparison; in surveys they

are the criteria implicit in the wording of the questions and the manner in which respondents understand those criteria. A common shortcoming of both kinds of studies is the failure to adequately describe these criteria and assess their impact. As a result it is often very difficult to evaluate the role of unintentional bias in the various findings.

Efforts to analyze and compare experiences from printed sources have varied considerably in the scope of their definitions. Most of the classics of the field, such as Evelyn Underhill's *Mysticism*, have focused on very intense experiences, often involving changes in perception, time sense, and so forth, and subjectively described as qualitatively different from ordinary experience. Depending on how these criteria are used, such studies have dealt with one or more of the traditional categories of mystical experience: nature mysticism, theistic mysticism, and monistic or soul-mysticism. These have heavily emphasized the reports of "career mystics." Another more recent trend has been to include the experiences of those intoxicated by hallucinogens. Early influential examples are William James's description of his own experience after inhaling nitrous oxide (*Varieties of Religious Experience*, pp. 378–79) and Aldous Huxley's experience with mescalin (*The Doors of Perception*). There are also older accounts of experiments with cannabis, hashish, and other drugs, but it was not until Timothy Leary made LSD famous that "drug induced mysticism" came to be most widely compared to nonintoxicated states, although the use of "mind altering" substances to

facilitate sacred experiences has long been a part
of many cultures. Research on psychedelic drug
experiences has strongly influenced the Perennial
Philosophy approach, presumably by encouraging
the conclusion that an experience that can be
naturally induced can also be naturally explained,
and also because psychedelic experience is well
known to be heavily shaped by psychological set
and cultural input. In these cases the definition of
the experience is more by its "trigger" than anything specific about the experience itself. Still
other efforts at comparison have included some
forms of mental illness (Huxley, for example, was
intrigued by apparent similarities between mania
and his mescalin experience), plus a variety of
other intense subjective events that are felt to be
more or less different from ordinary life experience. Of course, the wider the net has been cast,
the more the classic descriptions of religious mystical experience have been made to appear culture-
specific and relatively infrequent. This effect is
enhanced by the obvious fact that general experiences of intense emotion, esthetic pleasure, and so
forth are likely to be described in religious terms
by the religious and in nonreligious terms by the
nonreligious. We have all heard religious people
remark on seeing a beautiful sunset or a rainbow
that such an experience gives them certainty of
the existence of God, while on the other hand it
may give an atheist as much pleasure and even
awe without the slightest hint of supernatural
meaning.

When such ordinary experiences are included

in an analysis, "cultural loading" is certain to be found. But generalization from such analyses to mystical experience *per se* is unwarranted. Certain kinds of extraordinary events seem to suggest supernatural interpretations to those who experience them regardless of their prior beliefs; other kinds of extraordinary experiences, and ordinary ones as well, are interpreted almost entirely on the basis of prior belief.

Surveys of mystical experience, variously named and defined, are just as determined by the investigator's criteria as comparisons of preexisting written accounts, but they are even more difficult to interpret since the investigator's criteria interact with each respondent's criteria (often different) for the same words and phrases. Greeley's survey was unusual among recent studies in that its question was intentionally patterned on classic descriptions of religious mystical experience and was accompanied by a checklist of descriptors that allowed the investigators to select from among all positive respondents a subset who were clearly describing the religious mystical experience. The more typical approach is illustrated by a frequently cited study by Linda B. Bourke and Kurt W. Back, "Language, Society, and Subjective Experience." Using the term *transcendent experiences* (very broadly defined as "extremely intense experiences," p. 2) these investigators used two sets of questions intended to provide "esthetic language" and "religious language" for transcendent experiences in order to compare the social positions of respondents. An example of an esthetic question was:

"Have you ever seen or heard anything so beautiful that it made you indescribably happy or sad?" A religious question was: "Have you ever had a feeling of being saved in Christ?" According to the researchers the results of this study, involving 1,553 interviews, were "not as definitive as we might have hoped" (p. 17), but they still felt the data supported their hypothesis that "the experiences themselves are not different regardless of whether they are labelled as esthetic or religious" (p. 19). My own inclination is to conclude that such a hypothesis could never be definitively confirmed or disconfirmed without obtaining actual descriptions of the experiences from the subjects themselves, with special attention to separating the experiential features, that is the observations of the subjects, from their interpretations and the language used to express them.

The problem of whether we are dealing with one thing or more than one thing, and the role of language in that problem, is best illustrated for me by a natural experiment that I observed quite by accident a number of years ago. In 1973 I was teaching at Memorial University of Newfoundland, and that Christmas my wife and I held a party for the faculty and graduate students of my department. At the time, my parents were visiting us from the States. During the party I observed my mother and one of my students engaged in what appeared to be a very intense and enjoyable conversation that lasted for over half an hour. I later asked my mother what she and Monica had found to talk about for so long. She responded that they had been discussing New Brunswick. My mother had taught in New Brunswick in the 1930s and Monica had grown up in New Brunswick in the 1950s and 1960s. They were both very fond of the place and had greatly enjoyed talking about it. Not until I informed them—and I have never been quite sure whether this was a civilized thing to do—did they realize that while my mother was speaking of the city of New Brunswick, New Jersey, Monica had been speaking of the Canadian province of New Brunswick.

A great many words function as *New Brunswick* did in that conversation (the technical linguistic term for this is "polysemia"), and this phenomenon is a major source of the apparent consensus that characterizes our very heterogeneous culture. Imagine a survey that asked North Americans whether they had ever been in New Brunswick. If a description were elicited from those who claimed to have visited it, the results would appear quite odd to an investigator who knew *only* the city (or the province). One entire set of respondents would seem to be mistaken about part, but only part, of their description: either the majority of Canadians or the majority of Americans would seem to suffer from a culture-bound difficulty in getting the description just right. Perhaps it would be explained that Americans, with their widespread experience of urbanization, could not help emphasizing cities in their description of the largely rural province of New Brunswick. On the other hand, if the investigator were from New Jersey, he might feel it understandable that Canadians, accustomed as they

are to the wilderness, would recall the parks of
the city with such an inflated image. I am, in fact,
certain that much the same thing has been going
on in the effort to view all mystical experience as
of one kind and to explain away the "ethnocentric
phrasings" of it. And the barriers to open communication about such experiences, as described
above, have been enormously helpful in allowing
this confusion to persist. The more detailed and
highly structured a person's experience, the greater
the disincentives to revealing it unless one is a
member of a group (e.g., Charismatic Christians)
that sanctions both the experience and its sharing.
The effect, of course, is to increase further the appearance that only those who already believe in
such things experience them, when in fact it is
much more the case that only those who already
believe in such things are in a position to speak
freely about them.

VI

The best way to proceed in the examination of
this question is to look at a particular kind of
mystical experience that seems to suggest strongly
a variety of supernatural beliefs and about which
we have some evidence concerning its relationship
to culture. Fortunately, this is easier today than
it would have been a few years ago, because we
may now consider the "near death experience," or
NDE. But first a possible objection to using this as
an illustration must be overcome: some may not
consider it a mystical experience at all, especially
those who have been primarily interested in the

oceanic experience. On this score I shall simply point out that NDE's in most cases fit the definitions of *mystical* in general use, including the one from the *OED* quoted above, and that they are in every particular the kind of experience with which traditional writers on mysticism have concerned themselves.[8] Furthermore, in the research project described above, I found that Greeley's carefully worded mysticism question was very effective in eliciting reports of NDE's. I am not attempting to argue that NDE's are *the* mystical experience, still less that they are identical to the oceanic or nature mysticism experience of union. Many NDE's, though, do contain clear elements of a kind of union, and the case that I shall present here includes some of these. I have anticipated this objection primarily because current proponents of the Perennial Philosophy perspective have tended to look very disparagingly at NDE's. Comfort, for instance, lumps the entire subject under the heading of "Kübler-Ross shamanism" and asserts that NDE's "are just as common after incompetent dental work under nitrous oxide . . . as they are after near-death" ("On Going to the Forest," p. 37). Quite apart from the issue of whether the near-dental experiences here referred to are "the same" as NDE's, one must wonder whether William James, whose conversion to an appreciation of mystical experience came through the inhaling of nitrous oxide, would have understood this jibe, or how it relates

---

8. See, for example, Underhill, *Mysticism,* pt. 2, ch. 5, "Voices and Visions."

to the general tendency to accept experiences triggered by LSD and other chemicals. I suspect that this reluctance to deal with the typical NDE stems from the fact that its phenomenology, and the changed attitude toward death that it engenders, are distinctly supernaturalistic — and there is growing evidence that these features are not a simple result of culture-loading. Because those contents of experience that seem to indicate a supernatural reality have been primarily explained away by use of the culture-loading hypothesis, the appearance that some such contents are independent of culture (or at least cannot be connected with cultural factors in the straightforward ways that have traditionally been used) makes secular theorists rather uncomfortable.

It is worth stressing that the present point is not whether the supernatural interpretations and beliefs involved are true, nor whether the experiences genuinely involve contact with real supernatural beings and forces. I am instead concerned with whether such experiences constitute a distinct type of event rather than merely a variation on a kind of experience that would have appeared purely natural if not for the religious mind set and vocabulary of the subject. Such explanations have been proposed for the NDE in much the same way that they have been proposed for other religious mystical experiences, but they have not enjoyed the support of any notable empirical data.

The near death experience, as such, first came to public attention in 1975 when Raymond A. Moody published *Life After Life*. The book immediately became a huge success and has continued not only to sell but to spawn an entire genre of popular and academic publications. Moody claimed to have discovered that many people who have nearly died recall a remarkably complex pattern of subjective events. He illustrated this pattern with the following description of an "ideal case," noting that no person he had interviewed reported every feature mentioned, but that all of the features had been described repeatedly:

A man is dying and, as he reaches the point of greatest physical distress, he hears himself pronounced dead by his doctor. He begins to hear an uncomfortable noise, a loud ringing or buzzing, and at the same time feels himself moving very rapidly through a long dark tunnel. After this, he suddenly finds himself outside of his own physical body, but still in the immediate physical environment, and he sees his own body from a distance, as though he is a spectator. He watches the resuscitation attempt from his unusual vantage point and is in a state of emotional upheaval.

After a while, he collects himself and becomes more accustomed to his odd condition. He notices that he still has a "body," but one of a very different nature and with very different powers from the physical body he has left behind. Soon other things begin to happen. Others come to meet and to help him. He glimpses the spirits of relatives and friends who have already died, and a loving, warm spirit of a kind he has never encountered before — a being of light — appears before him. This being asks him a question, nonverbally, to make him evaluate his life and helps him along by showing him a panoramic, instantaneous playback of the major events of his life. At some point he finds himself approaching some sort of barrier or border, apparently representing the limit between earthly life and the next life. Yet, he finds that he must go back to the earth, that the time for his death has not yet come. At this point he resists, for by now he is taken up with his experiences in the afterlife and does not want to return. He is overwhelmed by intense feelings of joy, love, and peace. Despite his attitude, though, he somehow reunites with his physical body and lives.

Later he tries to tell others, but he has trouble doing so. In the first place, he can find no human words adequate to describe these unearthly episodes. He also finds that others scoff, so he stops telling other people. Still, the experience affects his life profoundly, especially his views about death and its relationship to life. (Pp. 23–24)

From this description it is obvious that several of the features most often included in even the highest form of mystical union experience, particularly of the religious variety, are present: "being lifted out of yourself" (no metaphor here, though!), supernal light, intense positive affect, and ineffability. To this we might add the reluctance to speak about the experience, also so frequently encountered among "ordinary mystics."

Reaction to Moody's book from professional quarters was decidedly skeptical. "If such a dramatic event were at all frequent, then surely we would all have known about it before now!" That very natural reaction is no longer tenable, not only for the NDE, but for a great variety of nonordinary experiences, as I have noted above. In fact, the ability of our society to prevent these things from being generally known may be one of the most extraordinary features of the subject.

I obtained the following case in a rather round-about manner, as is often true with such accounts. In 1980 a colleague happened to describe to his mother some of my work with nonordinary experiences. His mother replied that he should talk to his sister about her experience. He went to his sister, explained the nature of my interest, and asked what had happened to her and why he had never heard about it. The experience was in fact a classic NDE and, typically, she had told only a very few people. Recently she had read the accounts of others, and this sufficiently reduced her shyness on the subject for her to consent to an interview.

Ruth, as I shall call her, is a surgical nurse in her late thirties.[9] She is white, middle-class, and well educated. She suffers from a chronic illness that occasionally requires medical attention, and it was during a diagnostic procedure related to this illness that the NDE took place. I interviewed Ruth in her home and what follows is a verbatim transcript of portions of that interview:

Well I was having a fluorescein angiography for my heart and I was watching on the monitor. I was having a great deal of coronary spasm and the pain became so intense that I realized that I was losing consciousness. The pain was incredible, really just unbelievable. Every-

---

9. Because of the social stigma still attached to such experiences it is generally necessary to agree to disguise the identity of one's interview subjects. This is one reason that Gen's candor is so valuable.

thing was centered on the pain. I couldn't escape it, I couldn't divert my attention. It was just overwhelming.

And—what I'll do is recount it the way I remember it. It was strange, of course. The pain was incredible, and when the pain became the most intense I had a horrible ringing noise that reverberated and kept ringing and reverberating and it was—and I was not just in pain but I was frightened and uncomfortable. And I was rushing, I thought, through sort of a black tunnel. Actually it was more like a hallway, which sounds silly, but that's what it seemed to me. A hallway, a corridor. . . .

And then, as the ringing seemed to diminish, which it did suddenly, I realized that the pain was gone. And that was an overwhelming feeling of relief! And I realized that I had floated right out of—as this was happening—I came right out of the top of my head. Now I was lying on the operating table and my feet were that-a-way and I was looking down. I was sort of somewhere over my knees. I could see Doctor Smith and his associate and people that I knew working on me, and this seemed of almost no importance to me. I was, you know, I just observed it. But I had the most over-whelming feeling of—after the relief from the pain—I felt like I was swimming or floating in a lovely—I don't know. If you can imagine swimming in champagne that's what it was like. It was lovely!

And I thought I was going to bump into the operating room light. Now, I assisted in surgery twice a week a great deal of my professional career. My concern was not to get into their way and I thought, "Why I'll just float over the light." But then I found that I had become part of the light; the light was enveloping me. Now, as I did this there was a clock on the wall facing the operating table and I turned around and I was facing down, but as I watched them I could see the clock

at the same time. I was constantly aware of the time
because I knew that in a given amount of time there
would be brain damage. And of course, I was quite
aware of that.

Now the feeling I had besides the pleasurable one
was one of joy, just unconditional love is the only
thing I can think of. I just felt, well I never had a feeling like that before so it's difficult to describe, but unconditional love comes as close as anything. And I was
in communication then. I keep thinking about it in my
mind as "they." Now there was a central being and I
have a feeling that that being was male. It was nobody
I could identify by sight, it was just someone who read
my mind and I read his mind. And I say that as an
afterthought because at the time I just knew that we
weren't speaking. And the whole time I was in communication with this person there was like a Greek chorus
in the background of others who had no recognizable
features or anything, but they were definitely multiple
presences that I was aware of as I watched them resus-
citate me. Now, after all my years in medicine, I had
some clinical interest in this, but it was, you know, if
you've done anything twice—I mean simultaneously—it
was something I was aware of but it was not something
that I was concerned about.

Now, the communication I had with that presence
was one simply of—I felt that we discussed my life. But
I also felt that I never had to say anything. I didn't say
anything, he didn't say anything. And he understood
my motivation. If I did something that I thought might
have been questionable or naughty, in my childhood,
he knew what my motivation was.

I had three concrete thoughts in all this. One was
that he said to me "you've been a good girl." And two,
that it wasn't time. That "Ray and the children"—as a

group, not by individual name—"need you and it isn't time." And also the third thing which was such a strong, strong—command almost—was that suicide is something that you shouldn't contemplate, something you should never attempt and you should encourage others. It is almost incorrigible, you know. It is just unforgivable, practically.

OK, in the meantime, I'm watching what's going on and when he said to me it's time—I was so happy, and I wasn't even sure this was a good idea to go back to the body—but he said, you know, everything is fine and you should return, so I did. I was aware, as I regained consciousness, of this immense grin on my face. And Dr. Smith, who has been my physician for years and a dear friend, said, "Do you know what happened?" I said, "Yes, I died." And he answered, "You sure as hell did!" And I'm saying "Hi!" to everyone like I had just returned from a trip and I am joyous about this thing.

Ruth did not learn of Moody's book, and therefore the experiences of others, until a number of years after this event, yet there can be no doubt that her experience is remarkably consistent with the pattern that Moody first brought to our attention: physical distress, ringing noise, movement down a dark tunnel, detachment from the physical body, observation of resuscitation attempts, the "being of light," the life review conducted nonverbally, the feeling of love and joy, the preference not to return, the return to the physical body, the difficulty of description. Ruth's subsequent attempts to share the experience were also similar to those described by Moody and noted above in connection with all sorts of nonordinary experiences in our culture. On her way from the recovery room to her hospital room, Ruth tried to tell another nurse about what had happened, and was in fact rebuffed. Her colleague said that she did not like to hear about such things! Apart from her husband she told no others until much later. In fact, Ruth's experience is much more complete in its resemblance to Moody's "ideal case" than most that I have encountered, and I strongly suspect that we have underestimated the amount of interesting variety that exists among NDE's. Nonetheless, this pattern is fascinating and well established by empirical research. It also illustrates very well the questions that we have been dealing with in this essay.

Is this an "ethnocentric phrasing" of a generalized "peak experience"? Is it correct, as Robert S. Ellwood, Jr., has written, that "we can probably accept the theorem that no significant differences exist between . . . mystical and nonmystical ecstatic experiences, apart from those differences injected by interpretation," *(Mysticism and Religion,* p. 29)? This distinction between interpretation and observation is an excellent and important one, and it is implicit in several of the arguments reviewed above. However, when one has established such a wealth of complex subjective detail that is compellingly real to the subject, and that is so similar among the experiences of independent individuals, it becomes impossible to maintain that these are merely the effect of culturally provided religious interpretations on the description of a relatively undifferentiated feeling state.

At this point the Perennial Philosophy approach must drop back to an explanation that involves the cultural shaping of a complex hallucinatory state triggered by physiological mechanisms. In cases such as Ruth's and many others the mechanism would presumably be lack of oxygen. A typical example of this response appeared in 1977 in an editorial in the *Archives of Internal Medicine.* In "Afterthoughts on Afterlife," Samuel Vaisrub was critical of Moody, arguing that these near death experiences are easily explained by current knowledge. The author noted that it is not at all surprising that people in extreme physical distress should hallucinate, especially if they are anoxic; nor is it surprising that their hallucinations should have the appearance of wish fulfillments that help alleviate the fear of impending death. The contents of these hallucinations are somewhat similar, for obvious cultural reasons, he said, stating that "the picture is not unfamiliar to those who have seen similar representations of the hereafter in filmed Hollywood fantasies" (p. 150). Only the facts stand in the way of such a cultural explanation. The only film depicting the events described by Moody is *Beyond and Back,* produced in 1977 (Sunn Classic Pictures) and directly based on the concepts and materials in his book. Prior to the widespread popular interest aroused by the book, the set of events described by Ruth and others was generally unknown and certainly did not represent what one could call our culture's image of immortality. Although this difference between the specifics of the NDE and traditional images of life after death seems obvious, I did perform a small-scale survey in 1979 just to satisfy myself that I had not somehow overlooked a major cultural model. My sample consisted of twenty-two undergraduate students at a nearby college. They were all members of the same class; they were all born and raised in the eastern United States; and they were from a variety of Christian backgrounds. The small number of subjects does not warrant a more detailed analysis of their characteristics. In the first question I asked, "Do you believe in life after death?"; in the second question I requested a brief description of what they "would expect the experiences immediately following death to be like"; I then asked a series of questions about where they had received the impressions that they had just described. One student did not believe in life after death, a low percentage probably accounted for by the fact that this was a religiously affiliated school (Protestant). One other believed but had "no idea" what it would be like. The remaining twenty responses fell very neatly into two groups.

Twelve students gave descriptions that contained at least one detail given in Moody's book. Examples included: "floating above and going up a tunnel"; "a light that draws toward a heaven of some kind"; "feel part of life float from body, see relatives, light"; "be in space looking down on body"; "come out of body and float upward." Of these twelve, 100 percent cited as their source Moody's book (5), the Sunn Classics film (3), Elizabeth Kübler-Ross (2), or the popular press in general (4). All of those who cited more than one source included Moody's book among them.

The other eight students gave descriptions that do reflect traditional images from Western tradition. These included: "the rebirth of Paul"; "heavenly, peaceful, Kingdom of God"; "heaven—not really sure. It's a mystery—peace, love, and happiness in this Utopian community"; "having just switched worlds." Of these eight, one was unsure where the impressions had come from; one said that her impression came from people in general; and six cited some combination of "church," "my religion," and the Bible. None of these respondents cited Moody, Kübler-Ross, any motion picture, or the general popular press.

Although I have not extended this survey formally to a larger population, I have continued to find precisely the same association of images and sources among those whom I have interviewed concerning religious beliefs and experiences. Even those who have had their own NDE in the typical pattern are thoroughly surprised by the pattern and assume that their experience is unique unless or until they learn of the NDE literature. With the passage of time, of course, more and more people—both those with NDE's and those without them—have become familiar with this pattern. Nonetheless, while this indicates an extremely important shift in our culture's images of life after death, the events have proceeded in the wrong order for these images to "explain" the contents of NDE's. This is especially true now that historical and anthropological research have been brought to bear on the issue and have uncovered the same pattern in the distant past (there is, for instance, a good example in Plato's *Republic,* as Moody noted in *Life After Life,* pp. 82–84); and in other cultures (I have myself obtained a typical example, through an interpreter, from a Seminole Indian woman who spoke no English). The independence of the typical NDE experience from prior belief and from knowlcdge of the pattern has also been fully supported by excellent systematic research. Two of the clearest examples are *Life at Death* by Kenneth Ring, Ph.D., a psychologist, and *Recollections of Death* by Michael B. Sabom, M.D., a cardiologist.

Current knowledge about the NDE, then, supports and extends the following hypotheses about mystical experience: there are several distinct and coherent forms of such experience; in at least some of these forms, perceptions and information (James's noetic quality) are as important as feelings in the emotional sense; the characteristics of these forms of experience cannot be accounted for entirely on the basis of language or cultural input (although both are doubtless important); therefore, obviously, religious mystical experiences cannot be reduced to aberrant or localized forms of nonreligious mystical or ecstatic experiences. Furthermore, the sudden "discovery" of the NDE illustrates again the fact that the conventional reductionistic approach has done more to suppress information and retard the growth of our knowledge about mystical experience than to scientifically explain it.

Ruth's case is not only useful for this general discussion of mystical experience, but also has some special relevance to Gen's experience. To fully appreciate the connections it is necessary to return to my interview with Ruth and consider two experiences that she had several months after her NDE.

RUTH: I got awake in bed with chest pain. As I was taking my nitroglycerine I took a drink of water, because you're frequently thirsty, and I didn't feel like I could go back to sleep. But I closed my eyes and I thought, "Gee, the moon is bright tonight." I opened my eyes and there was a light in my bedroom. Now, it was a very bright, very—almost as if you would stare at one of your television lights. [The interview was videotaped, and this referred to one of our spotlights. DH] It had no shape, it had no substance, but I felt terrifically relieved and I thought about my experience and I thought, "That's very foolish for me to be concerned about my health. Obviously I'm going to be all right," and I went to sleep. I know how this sounds. I even hate to recount but it really—.

DH: You saw the light, and you felt that you shouldn't worry about your health?

RUTH: Well, it was more than just the light. It was once again this feeling of love—joy! It's an *incredible* sensation, and there is nothing that I've ever experienced that is quite like it. It's the way, it's almost the way I felt when they brought me my babies. I felt towards that child, that's the way the world is towards me. I felt this overabundance of love, and warmth. "There

143

are no problems; everything is fine." That's the only way I know to describe it. And all I was aware of was this light. And I—and the feeling, of course, which is an overwhelming sensation.

DH: Did you feel that you were definitely awake?

RUTH: Oh, yes, yes, because I sleep on three pillows so my head is elevated, and I actually swung my legs off of the side and sat up in bed. And readjusted my pillows and I thought this light was the moon and that's when I got a different perspective.

DH: You were sitting up?

RUTH: Oh, yes.

DH: Where in the room was the light?

RUTH: Right at the side of the bed. Like I could almost touch it.

DH: Was the light localized?

RUTH: Yes, well it was brighter in the center, but it was—it was large. It didn't have a definite shape. I wouldn't have called it a ball.

DH: How large would you say?

RUTH: Maybe—it was more oval than anything. It was like four feet tall, but it was floating. It wasn't down on the carpet. It was up.

DH: About how wide was it?

RUTH: I don't know. Maybe two feet.

DH: How far above the carpet was it?

RUTH: It was higher than the side of the bed.

DH: On which side of the bed?

RUTH: On the right side. As if someone were standing at the side of the bed. But, it wasn't a person and it wasn't a shape. It was just a light. And it was there a long time. I mean when I first looked at it I thought the moon was bright and then I thought, "Now this is strange." When I swung my legs off of the bed it stayed where it was and just sort of got larger. It sort of came towards me or got larger. I don't know which.

DH: So you saw the light while you were lying down and when you sat up it seemed to get larger?

RUTH: Yes. And then I was made aware that it wasn't the moon and it was obviously a light that was in the room with me.

DH: Was the room dark except for the light?

RUTH: Oh, yes, totally.

DH: Were you able to see things in the room by this light? Did it cast shadows?

RUTH: Well, it just kind of—well, it's like your eyes adjusting to the light. It really wasn't like a light coming on in the bedroom. It was nothing like that. And I really wasn't even interested in anything else except what I had just done. I knew that I was awake; I had just taken my pills which means I have to unscrew the bottle, shake them out, put them under my tongue. I had taken a drink of water and rearranged the pillows and this light was still there and that's when it—that's when I settled back.

DH: And did you say how long you thought it was there?

RUTH: Oh, perhaps five minutes. I didn't go to sleep right away.

DH: You laid back down with it still there then?

RUTH: Well, yes. As a matter of fact I closed my eyes and opened them and it was still there. So probably longer than five minutes.

DH: Was it still there when you went to sleep?

RUTH: Yes. I had the feeling that it was watching over me. That's—that's just the feeling I had.

DH: And so it made you comfortable about going to sleep?

RUTH: Yes.

DH: Did you have the feeling that this light was a person, that it had a personality?

RUTH: Yes. It definitely was part of the same experience that I had before. I was in really acute distress. I had been taking Demerol for the chest pain, and I take that only when I must. I hadn't taken any at that time because I was getting better. When I woke up I was in severe pain, but I'd been in pain for days. I wasn't particularly concerned. I'd been through this before and I knew I'd get better, but the pain was severe and I was unhappy. When the light came, even though I had some residual chest pain, I felt that it wasn't anything to be concerned about. I don't know how to explain it.

DH: Did the pain seem different after the light came? Were you in less pain?

RUTH: Yes. Well, of course I had taken my nitroglycerine. So there's no way to measure that, except to say I did go to sleep and eventually—. But I was awake—you asked me—I'm sure that light was still there when I went to sleep. Yes.

DH: Then you immediately connected this with your previous experience?

RUTH: Yes. Because of the feeling.

DH: Did you associate the light with the personality with which you thought you had communicated?

RUTH: Yes. You'll remember that I said that at first I thought the light was the operating room light because they're quite bright and large, and over you when you're in the operating theater. . . .

DH: Did the light in the operating room continue or did it have a separateness? Was it *a* light in the way that the light in the bedroom was *a* light?

RUTH: Yes. And it was the *same* light, the same general—. Its shape, it doesn't have—I could not describe to you any features that we would recognize as human, for example. Nothing like that. It was more a *feeling* than a visual thing.

DH: And the experience in the bedroom—experience number two now—did you have any of the other feelings that you did in the first one? Any feeling of communication, for example?

RUTH: No. No. Except that I felt well. I mean I had such a sense of wellbeing and love and, and—. The only—. To say there was any communication, I think the only thing I can say is that I had the idea that everything was going to be all right. That's all I mean.

DH: In the first one you said that you had the feeling that the personality that you were with was masculine. Did you have a similar feeling in the second experience?

RUTH: Yes. Yes.

DH: But that was the only characteristic?

RUTH: Yes. [Long pause.] And that may be an enculturated thought. You know. It's hard to say.

DH: Now, I believe you said that you had had two after the one in the hospital.

RUTH: Well, I had another experience with the light which was almost identical to the first. And again it was at a time when my physical condition was very poor and was almost identical. There was no change, as a matter of fact, except that this time I stayed awake afterwards and I read. When my husband got awake, stirred,

I spoke to him and I told him about it, because I wanted to make sure I wasn't asleep.

DH: Then in that one you remained awake until the light left?

RUTH: Yes. And it just, it just receded. It didn't just vanish. It just sort of slowly got dimmer, but it left me with the feeling of well-being.

DH: When you say it got dimmer, do you mean that it just gradually went away without moving off through space?

RUTH: Yes. It didn't seem to get—. It didn't seem to get smaller or move off through space. It just got dimmer.

DH: Until you were no longer able to see it?

RUTH: Yes.

Most discussion and research concerning NDE's has been very tightly focused on the small portion of time, typically a matter of minutes, during which the basic experience takes place. Recently there has also been interest in the long-term consequences of these experiences, for example, changed attitudes toward death. However, there has been very little investigation of subsequent nonordinary experiences in the lives of those who have had NDE's. Ruth's is one of several cases I have encountered that suggest this as a fruitful direction in which to expand our inquiries. Various kinds of connections are possible between such experiences and the NDE's that may have preceded them. These range from the possibility that the events of the NDE may somehow produce a facility for subsequent visionary experiences (I consider this unlikely) to the virtual certainty that subsequent experiences will be interpreted by the subject in the light of previous experiences felt to be similar. In Ruth's case the connections appear to be very strong.

Ruth's second and third experiences are good examples of the more general kind of mystical experience, in contrast to the transcendent experience of union of which the NDE appears to be a variety. However, they share with her NDE the fact that the events permitted her only two possible kinds of interpretation: either she was somehow imagining the experience, or it was supernatural. It is clear that for Ruth only the latter option was felt to be really viable. Nonetheless, she is typical of most whom I have interviewed in that, despite her previous experience, she did initially consider the possibility that she was dreaming and took a variety of measures to test this hypothesis before rejecting it. She even attempted to distinguish between her "enculturated" interpretations and direct observation. The academic literature on supernatural belief generally implies that believers of all kinds leap to their supernatural conclusions; that their desire to find the transcendent in the ordinary prevents adequate reality testing and fills common events with uncommon significance. This may be true for some people in some situations. However, when "weird" experiences occur in the lives of ordinary people I have found it much more the rule that all plausible naturalistic explanations that occur to the individual are tried out before the supernaturalistic ones are even considered. Of course, with such experiences as those that Ruth has had, it does not take long to exhaust the obvious naturalistic explanations. Quickly it seems that the only question left is whether or not to trust one's sanity.

Ruth, like Genevieve Foster, was not practicing any formal religion at the time of her experiences. Neither did she consciously hold any particular spiritual or supernatural beliefs. In fact, she had felt generally alienated from her Protestant upbringing. The experiences themselves served to convince her of the reality of a spiritual realm and, as is almost universally the case with NDE's, of the personal immortality of humans. In these ways we may say that her experiences made her "more religious." However, and this is also typical of such experiences, it did not cause her to become more formally religious; that is, she did not decide to join a church as a result of the experiences.[10] Those who are formally religious to begin with are likely to assimilate their mystical experiences to their formal religious framework. This is not difficult in all except the most secularized religious settings or in denominations that have very specific teachings relevant to such experiences (e.g., Jehovah's Witnesses and Seventh Day Adventists believe that immediately following death there is a dreamless sleep that lasts until

---

10. On this aspect of NDE's see Ring, *Life at Death*, ch. 9, "Aftereffects II: Attitudes Toward Religion and Death." For a study that suggests a significant relationship between reported mystical experience in general and formal religious behavior see Ralph W. Hood, Jr., "Mystical Experience as Related to Present and Anticipated Future Church Participation."

the Final Judgment and the End of Time). After
all, while these experiences do not reflect the specific contents of traditional Western religious
teachings, neither do they contradict them. The
fact that those who are not formally religious do
not tend to become so, despite a major increase in
personal religiosity, probably reflects the tendency
of most Christian denominations today either to
make no comment about such experiences or to
regard them with a combination of suspicion and
embarrassment.

The profoundly religious sense imparted by
these experiences, and the intimacy of the feelings
aroused, is partly responsible for the reluctance of
those who experience them to discuss them in the
modern intellectual climate. It is not just that
they do not wish to be treated as insane. They
also do not wish to have their most precious personal memories subjected to sneers. But, in addition to contributing to restraint, this strongly religious feeling frequently moves people, under the
right circumstances, to speak out on the matter to
help someone else. In Ruth's case this happened
when a close friend of her sister's died. In talking
with her sister and realizing how shattered she
was by the loss, Ruth decided that knowledge of
the NDE would be of specific and direct help. She
told her about the experience, with the assurance
that death was not an ending or a permanent parting, and found that it did indeed help her sister
through a difficult time. This is the dimension of
mystical experience about which we know the least,
but which is in a sense the most important. How

do these experiences fit into a person's subsequent life, and most particularly how do they enter into the subject's relationships with others? We know something of this in those cultures whose institutions are still open to religious experience, but we know almost nothing about its hidden effect in our modern, secularized age. This is part of the beauty of Gen's memoir. Her experience is placed within the context of an entire lifetime, and the memoir itself is a response to the same impulse that led Ruth to risk vulnerability and tell her sister what had happened to her and what she believed it meant. Gen has done all of us an enormous favor by her willingness to do the same *in public.*

VII

Now let us turn to a consideration of Gen's account in particular and examine its relationship to what has just been said about mystical experience in general. In doing this I shall include material drawn from my interviews with Gen and from the unpublished family letters that she has graciously shared with me. I should add that Gen has read this entire essay and has commented on many of the points that I have made. I certainly do not want to claim that she therefore shares responsibility for all of my arguments and conclusions or that my analysis of her experience is precisely the one that she would offer. However, through our discussions we have reached a consensus that includes the important matter of how her Jungian perspective relates to her understanding of what happened to her.

The long-standing academic tendency to explain mystical experience in psychopathological terms is certainly not supported by Gen's case. In fact, she gives eloquent testimony that in her own estimation the experience marked an important and persistent enhancement of her psychological well-being.

Gen's account is also helpful with the question of whether mystical experiences are a single kind of "altered state" whose appearance of variation is the result of available language (religious words versus naturalistic words) and the subject's culturally provided interpretive framework. To bring the memoir to bear on this issue, however, we must first deal with the relationship of the Jungian perspective to mysticism and religion. Jungian psychology has from its inception concerned itself with the religions of mankind, with special emphasis on the patterns found among religious expressions from different cultures. This attention to religion has been seen as a major strength by the adherents of Jungian thought. From those who have opposed Jung's theories this emphasis has drawn censure, and Jung himself was at times criticized for being a mystic. For our purposes, the most important element in this contention is the Jungian idea of the "collective unconscious," and the "archetypes" that Jung described as residing there.

The contents of the collective unconscious are advanced in Jungian thought as, in part, an explanation of many of the apparent universals in religious experience and expression (as well as the experiences that occur in dreams, psychotic states, and other altered states of consciousness). Contact with the collective unconscious is presented as having the potential for either great good or great harm for the individual, depending on the individual's response. This is perhaps evident from the caution that Gen describes among her Jungian acquaintances on such points as the idea of creating a "group mandala" and on the most appropriate response to her vision. What is often *not* clear to the uninitiated, and what often appears to vary from one Jungian to another, is whether the collective unconscious is the repository of a sort of "racial memory" that is "collective" in the sense that each individual has one that is basically like that possessed by all other individuals, or, on the other hand, the collective unconscious is "collective" in the sense of being somehow transpersonal, that is, having some sort of existence separate from the individual whose consciousness and personal unconscious are influenced by it. This is, of necessity, a great oversimplification, but it serves to highlight one of the most important points in the application of Jungian thought to religion.

If everyone carries within his own brain an inherited body of potential religious patterns that is identical to those inherent in the brains of all other humans, this collection could be used to explain at least large parts of religious experience and belief in psychological terms. If, for instance, many people around the world claim to have encountered God directly through mystical experience and even describe God and the experience in very complex and very similar ways, and even if these people can be shown not to have been mutually influenced by similar cultural input with regard to God and mystical experience, these similar patterns will have little value as evidence of religious truths *per se* if they are shown to result from *inborn* commonalities in human potentials for religious thought. In effect this perspective provides a means for explaining much or all of religious experience in purely psychological terms.

If, on the other hand, the collective unconscious is viewed as being transpersonal in the sense of having an existence separate from the subject, then it becomes analogous to the mystical concept of the Ground of the Soul, that immortal part of the human that transcends the natural and temporal order and participates in pure Being. In this case the collective unconscious appears as a means by which much of psychology may be explained in religious terms. All psychodynamic language tends to be heavily symbolic and metaphorical, so it is often difficult to be certain of what a writer intends to convey about what is *really* real, a redundancy necessitated by the psychodynamic concern with a multiplicity of frames of reality including purely subjective ones. Of all psychodynamic language Jungian language is the most symbolic and metaphorical, so the exact theological importance of Jungian concepts is generally very difficult to pin down, even for a single writer.

Fortunately what is most important for us is the precise meaning of one person, Genevieve Foster, when she uses Jungian language to describe and interpret her mystical experience. And this is a subject that she and I have talked about at length. As noted above, many scholars of mystical experience have assumed that available language and frames of interpretation operate exclusively to assimilate fundamental experience to the local intellectual climate; that these factors transmute the fundamental experience into what Maslow called "ethnocentric phrasings." Comfort summed up this point succinctly when he said that the natural event is given supernatural appearance when, in a religious culture the mystic makes "the religious noises appropriate to the culture."[11] From this point of view, language and interpretive frames (with the obvious exception of the particular author's language and interpretation) are primarily seen as obstacles to a clear and realistic view of the experience and its "true" meaning. In examining Gen's account (or, in fact, anyone's account) I would argue that this approach is excessive. To the extent that we feel the core experience to be both important and to some extent describable, it is necessary to strive to appreciate separately the domains of experience, language, and interpretation. Having done our best with this we are better equipped to understand the integration of all three domains. The mystic's language and interpretation present challenges to the scholar, but they are also profoundly important and redolent of meaning.

Concerning Jungian theory, my impression is that Gen's view of the collective unconscious is in

---

11. See my discussion in section 3 above.

important ways a religious one. She told me, for
example, "I think the collective unconscious is
something that we share with everybody else.
There's a connection. It's a pool that we all draw
from, I should say." After noting that she was not
attempting to speak authoritatively for Jungian
psychology she added that "our ability to have a
religious experience depends on whatever metaphor our feeble intelligence can grasp, because our
sense of reality isn't that good." This is very close
to the classic mystical doctrine concerning visions: because spirit is itself invisible, the appearance of spiritual realities to human beings in this
life always involves the provision of some sort of
symbol.

Beyond her basic Jungian orientation, Gen has
made it very clear that her own experience is one
that she sees as religious in the fullest sense of
the word. When she originally circulated her
memoir to her family, long before she had thought
of publication, she noted that for some of them it
would be hard to understand. She said of one
loved one in particular, and of a certain Jungian
author, "you have gone to the farthest reaches of
mythology, but neither you nor he makes the leap
into religious experience. Bear with me if you
can." Then, toward the end of that original document, she reflected back on what she had written
and made the following closing statement: "These
ideas are only fantasies. When you have abandoned any and all creeds, all you have left are fantasies to tell you the nature of the unseen world.
But I have learned over a long lifetime to take my

fantasies seriously. *As for the experience of intellectual vision that I had in mid-life, that was not
fantasy, that was an experience of Reality, so that
I can say with Jung, I do not believe, I know"* (my
emphasis).

It is not surprising that Gen describes and
discusses her experience in Jungian terms, as a
Roman Catholic might describe and discuss it in
Catholic terms. However, her Jungian outlook did
not demand a religious, or even a positive, interpretation of the vision. Gen has told us of the
broadly negative reaction of her analyst, Dr. Harding, to those creative elements that she sees as
most relevant to the understanding of her mystical experience, and of Dr. Harding's advice to mistrust the experience itself. She has also told me
that soon after the experience she spoke of it with
two friends, both of them Jungian analysts. She
said that "they were agreeably willing to listen,
but I didn't get much feedback from either one of
them," and in her memoir she writes that from
them she got "no real understanding; to them such
a thing seemed a sort of psychic curiosity, a side
issue, not really related to the business of development" (pp. 44–45). Whatever Jung himself might
have said, then, and in spite of the attention to
mythological symbols, she found that Jungian
thought did not encourage or support full-scale
mystical experience.

Gen's own religious background was even more
inhospitable to mystical experience. In her memoir
she says that it "was so far from my expectation,
so far from anything that I had thought in the

realm of the possible, that it has taken me the
rest of my life to come to terms with it" (p. 36),
and "occurring as it did to one reared in the most
staid and unemotional branch of Protestantism,
taught to believe that such things were truly
impossible, or if not impossible then certainly
abnormal—such an event was truly overwhelming" (p. 42). In the document that she originally
circulated to her family, Gen went even further,
speaking of her lack of official religious affiliation
since adolescence. "The reason that I don't go to
church is that none of the existing creeds work for
me anymore—but it is the creed, not the ritual,
that puts me off. The Episcopal ritual, or the
Catholic, or even the silence of the Friends' meeting house—they all speak to me. God is not dead,
but the mythology in which we did our thinking
has lost its potency and fallen apart—not for
everybody, but for me and for many others." Her
religious language and interpretation, then, are not
produced by a need to conform to the vernacular
of a religiocentric culture as exponents of the Perennial Philosophy approach would predict. They
are in fact presented despite the overwhelmingly
secular cultural context within which the experience occurred.

The next question that arises is the extent to
which Gen's language and interpretation, whatever
their origin, reflect elements that are intrinsic to
her experience. The description of her vision
clearly illustrates that, while such experiences are
impossible to describe completely, there are certain very specific things that *can* be communi-

cated. The basic describable features of her "intellectual vision" are:

1. the certainty of the presence of a person, complete with a spatial location,
2. the absence of any sensory cues relating to that person,
3. the wordless communication of a two-way flood of love with that person,
4. the bathing of her world with a nonphysical *light,*
5. the persistence of the experience for five days.

The matter of the presence, the presence that was so strongly felt to be a person, is crucial. In fact, the matter of disembodied persons is a central point of religious systems. It distinguishes religion from magic (the manipulation of supernatural forces), and it differentiates religious mystical experiences from the "oceanic" and nature-mystical experiences that scholars like Maslow and Comfort have considered the fundamental, "real," mystical experiences. Gen did not simply feel oneness with the universe and assume this must involve a person—God—because she had been taught that an infinite person was immanent in the universe. Rather, she had believed that there were no such persons and would have been much less astonished had she had a mere oceanic experience.

For many skeptics the matter of persons is the central problem with religion and with supernatural belief in general. In 1955 George Price summed up this response rather neatly in an article entitled "Science and the Supernatural." He

Commentary

posed the question of how a scientist ought to react to the report of an extraordinary phenomenon; whether the scientist should be "narrow-minded or receptive." His answer was: "The test is to attempt to imagine a detailed mechanistic explanation. Whenever we can imagine any sort of detailed explanation without introducing incorporeal intelligences, we should be prepared to regard the phenomenon open-mindedly. For this test it is not necessary that our explanation be simple, reasonable, or usable in making predictions" (p. 361). The crucial thing is that it should not involve "incorporeal intelligences." It is with the belief in nonphysical persons, then, that we find a most important modern boundary. Without persons an apparently supernatural phenomenon may well be reducible to an as yet unknown natural process. With the introduction of persons not bound by physical laws, not even possessing a physical existence and yet persons still, one has undeniably crossed into a new sort of domain, the supernatural domain postulated by religion.

Gen's "presence" was not only nonphysical but possessed no sensory attributes at all. This is one of the elements that has been so difficult for visionaries to describe to the rest of us. Nonetheless it turns out to be a relatively widespread phenomenon and has been discussed in both the mystical and the medical literature. In a useful medical article, C. Thompson has proposed designating this experience by the German word *Anwesenheit* (literally meaning "presence"). Thompson gives the following definition: "the subject, in clear con-

161

sciousness, suddenly becomes aware of another person in the immediate vicinity, although the subject may in reality be alone, or in the company of others. The extra person is not seen, heard or felt" (*"Anwesenheit,"* p. 628). He goes on to note that the experience is characterized by an "overriding sense of reality," that amounts to "an 'imposed sense of conviction.'" The phenomenon of which Thompson is speaking conforms quite perfectly to the "presence" element in Gen's experience. He reviews the reports of *Anwesenheit* in five contexts that have been described in the medical and psychological literature—bereavement, stressful isolation (as among polar explorers and ship-wrecked sailors), temporal lobe epilepsy, "sleep disturbances," and psychosis—and adds a sixth category of "drug-induced *Anwesenheit*" which he illustrates with two cases of patients receiving levodopa therapy for Parkinson's disease.

This review of what appear to be genuinely the same subjective experience in a variety of settings immediately raises again the twin questions of psychopathology and ultimate meaning. The presences experienced during bereavement are a part of the mounting evidence concerning a transcultural, experiential base for at least a part of the universally found belief in "ghosts" noted above (p. 122). Thompson says that the phenomenon "is such a common occurrence in this situation that it merits inclusion among the manifestations of normal grieving" (p. 629). In fact, several studies strongly suggest that these experiences have a positive effect and are a good prognostic sign in bereavement (see especially Greeley and Rees).

162

Commentary

The "sleep disturbance" cases noted by Thompson are the same as those that I discussed earlier in connection with traditions of supernatural assault (section 4). He mentions them in connection with the sleep disorder narcolepsy, a connection generally made in the medical literature, but the victims of these attacks are equally common in the normal population. In contrast to Gen's "loving presence," this class of experience is uniformly terrifying. A classic description of this kind of presence is given by William James in his *Varieties of Religious Experience* as told by a friend of his:

After I had gotten into bed . . . I lay awake thinking— when suddenly I *felt* something come into the room and stay close to my bed. It remained only a minute or two. I did not recognize it by any ordinary sense, and yet there was a horribly unpleasant sensation connected with it. It stirred something more at the roots of my being than any ordinary perception. . . . I was conscious of its departure as of its coming . . . The certainty that there in outer space stood something was indescribably stronger than the ordinary certainty of companionship when we are in the close presence of ordinary living people. The something seemed close to me and intensely more real than ordinary perception. (Pp. 59–60)

I have found this sensation of presence to be one of the most common elements of the sleep-paralysis–classic-nightmare experience, although it is often accompanied or replaced by the victim's actually seeing or hearing a terrifying figure. The sensation of presence, in fact the whole experience, is characterized by the overriding impression of reality noted by Thompson, and this is no doubt one of the major reasons that it is associated with beliefs about malevolent supernatural beings in cultures all over the world. My conclusion is that although it seems at times to co-occur with certain kinds of sleep related disorders, it must in general be considered as lying within the range of normal experience.

The sensation of presence that is related to stressful isolation (Thompson calls it *"Explorer's Anwesenheit"*) is interesting in view of the practice in some mystical traditions of living an isolated life of a severely penitential nature, either in a monastic cell or in the wilderness. It could be plausibly argued that such conditions can produce altered states of consciousness, perhaps even transient psychotic states. If so, then the sensation of presence in these settings may be generated by the same mechanism (or mechanisms) that produces it in the frankly pathological conditions of epilepsy, psychosis, and drug intoxication.

Some of these classes of the sensation of presence, then, appear associated with disease, others do not, and some may in fact be associated with an essentially healthy response. Thompson comments on this, saying that "the widely varying situations described above might suggest that diagnostically it is of little importance. Indeed it may be a more widespread experience, occurring in situations other than those described" (p. 630). Indeed, it may.

What does the connection between such presences and certain cases of specific pathology tell us about their ultimate significance? As with the

analogy between mystical experience and psychosis, and with the use of hallucinogens to induce
what many consider to be authentic mystical experience, the pattern is equivocal. If we found
such experiences exclusively in the presence of de-
monstrable disease or intoxication it would be
strong evidence against the mystic's claim that
they possess a significance beyond the purely subjective. If they were never found in the presence
of disease or intoxication this would effectively in-
validate the pathological interpretation that has
been so frequently argued. However, the consistent similarity of the phenomenon across both
cultural and pathological boundaries raises very
complicated questions for both schools of thought.
As Thompson notes at the end of his article, "a
necessary and sufficient cause for *Anwesenheit* is
unlikely to be forthcoming in the near future"
(p. 630).

The impressive consistency of the experience
of presences, and the manner in which Gen's experience conforms to the mystical norm, is further
enhanced by reference to the mystical literature.
We can probably do no better than examine the
sources to which she herself turned in trying to
determine whether what was happening to her
was unique: Evelyn Underhill's *Mysticism*, and
The Interior Castle of St. Teresa of Avila as
quoted therein. In chapter 8 of "The Sixth Mansions" St. Teresa describes the experience as being
sometimes that of the presence Jesus Christ Himself, and sometimes that of the saints. As seen in
Gen's description and the summaries just given,

165

the sensation of presence often includes some very specific "information" such as location, motion, gender, and so forth, even though there are no "appearances" associated with it. St. Teresa's knowledge that the presence is one or another specific person is therefore not so surprising. In this book St. Teresa is writing for contemplatives, that is, career mystics, who she expects may encounter this experience, and she wishes that they "may not be alarmed if any of these favours are granted you" (p. 180). Her description is well worth quoting.

> For example, a person who is no way expecting such a favour nor has even imagined herself worthy of receiving it, is conscious that Jesus Christ stands by her side although she sees Him neither with the eyes of the body nor of the soul. This is called an intellectual vision; I cannot tell why. I knew a person to whom God granted both this grace and others I shall describe later on. At first it distressed her greatly, for she could not understand it as she could see nothing, yet so convinced was she that Jesus Christ was thus in some way manifesting Himself that she could not doubt that it was some kind of vision, whether it came from God or no. Its powerful effects were a strong argument that it was from Him; still she was alarmed, never having heard of an intellectual vision, nor was she aware that such a thing could be. (Pp. 180–81)

The "person" of whom St. Teresa speaks here is herself, and this is her standard method of self-reference. It is done, at least in part, to avoid spiritual pride, a danger against which all the great mystics constantly caution, especially in connection with spiritual favors such as visions. So much so that, as St. Teresa comments a little later in this chapter, "This grace, if made good use of, prepares one receiving it to become a great servant of God, but sometimes our Lord bestows it on the weakest of souls; therefore in itself it is neither to be esteemed nor condemned. We must look to the virtues; she who is most mortified, humble and conscientious in serving God is the most holy" (pp. 186–87). Gen expressed this danger to me in psychological terms, saying that "if the ego engulfs this kind of experience, if *you* are the important thing—Look at me, *I've* had this kind of experience,—you may wind up in a locked ward."

Concerning the companionship of other presences St. Teresa says:

At times we may enjoy the company of some saint, which also brings us great profit. You will ask me, if the soul sees no one, how can it know whether it is Christ, or his most glorious Mother, or a saint? Such a person cannot answer this question or know how she distinguishes them, but the fact remains undoubted. It seems easy to recognize our Lord when He speaks, but it is surprising how the soul can, without hearing a word, recognize a saint who is silent and who seems sent by God to be its companion and helper. (Pp. 183–84)

The tremendous similarity between this experience as described by St. Teresa and by Gen is made even more striking by St. Teresa's observation that this kind of vision "does not pass away quickly but lasts for several days" (p. 181). In fact, the similarity is so great that one might be tempted to ascribe a large part of the similarity to Gen's reading quotations by St. Teresa in Underhill's *Mysticism* while she was in the midst of her own experience, plus the effect of the passage of forty years, were it not for the fact that this pattern is widespread regardless of prior knowledge. Thompson and others have noted that the identity of the presence is at times felt with great certainty, as St. Teresa says. This is especially common in cases of presences during bereavement, and of course when St. Teresa refers to the "saints" she is using a term that refers simply to those deceased persons believed to be in Heaven. Another striking parallel to St. Teresa's description can be easily given from the account of the experience of William James's friend, given above: "the certainty . . . was indescribably stronger than the ordinary certainty of companionship when we are in the close presence of ordinary living people." St. Teresa says that she was aware of this presence "being at her right hand, although not in the way we know an ordinary person to be beside us but in a more subtle manner which cannot be described. Yet this presence is quite as evident and certain, indeed far more so" (p. 182).

Evelyn Underhill confirms St. Teresa's description of "intellectual vision," saying that "although unseen of the eyes, it can be located in space. The mystic's general awareness of the divine is here focused upon one point—a point to which some theological or symbolic character is at once attached. The result is a sense of presence . . . concrete, defined and sharply personal" (p. 283).

The term *intellectual vision,* of which St. Teresa did not know the source, and which may have a confusing sound to the modern ear, was coined by St. Augustine (354–430 A.D.) to describe what he considered one of the three basic forms of vision, speaking of ordinary as well as extraordinary vision. He uses the term to refer to a "reality which can be perceived by the intellect alone" (*The Essential Augustine,* p. 95). In this he is distinguishing intellectual vision from visionary sensations and images. Always concerned with distinguishing the real from the illusory and the divine from the deceptive, mystics have generally regarded the intellectual vision as more real and more trustworthy than those visions in which images are seen, words are heard, and so forth. This is an interesting element in the mystical consensus since, to those of us who have never had such an experience, there is at first a tendency to assume that a "sense of presence" must be more vague and possess less impact than an experience in which one believes one sees someone nearby and hears him speak. But among those who have had the experience the reverse is true.

The variations of the sense of presence as categorized by Thompson, and even more the existence of a class of "presences" that are terrifying, shows that this is a motif that by itself does not constitute a form of experience with any specific significance—either from a medical or a mystical point of view. The pattern and the significance of an experience including such a sense of presence involves additional features. Apart from a certainty of the identity of the presence, an element that

Gen did not encounter, the most important additional element is the emotional tone that accompanies it.

For Gen the emotional tone was not merely positive, it was specifically the feeling of "interchange, a flood, flowing both ways, of love" (p. 43). This is a feeling often encountered in mystical experience. It is useful to compare this with Ruth's description of her "near death experience" that I quoted above. She said the feeling was "one of joy, just unconditional love is the only thing I can think of" (p. 136). And again, "It was once again this feeling of love—joy! It's an *incredible* sensation, and there is nothing that I've ever experienced that is quite like it. . . . I felt this overabundance of love, and warmth" (p. 143). Both descriptions conform to the classic descriptions of this sense of love in emphasizing that it "flows both ways." During this experience the mystic does not merely feel loved, nor merely feel terribly loving. The mutuality and the reciprocity of this love make a strong impression on the mystic, perhaps because this is one of the ways in which it is so unlike the imperfect experiences of mundane love.

Closely associated with the element of love is the impression of "light." Gen said, "There was light everywhere. . . . the world was flooded with light, the supernal light that so many of the mystics describe" (p. 43). And as she went about her ordinary business in this extraordinary atmosphere, keeping "her nose to the grindstone," she remained aware of "that glory blazing all around me" (p. 44). She reemphasized this element in our discussions. "I do recall this impression of *light*. You know, there was more light, as if the room were suffused with light. And yet I realized that it was not a physical impression. . . . It was illuminated, and yet I knew this also was an interior impression. It was not a physical sensation." Again, the comparison to Ruth's experience is inescapable, although in Ruth's, as is typical of the NDE, the light was directly associated with the person, what has often been described as a "being of light." In her first experience she says, "I found that I had become a part of the light; the light was enveloping me" (p. 135). Kenneth Ring, a psychologist and the first academic to carry out and publish truly systematic research on the NDE, found "Seeing the Light" and "Entering the Light" to be two of the five fundamental elements in the experience. He also found them to be the deepest, that is, the ones that were connected with the most complete and most positive experiences, and those of longest duration (*Life at Death*, pp. 30–66).

In connection with her subsequent experiences, Ruth tried to give more detail about the light. "I closed my eyes and I thought, 'Gee, the moon is bright tonight.' I opened my eyes and there was a light in my bedroom. . . . it was very bright. . . . It had no shape, it had no substance, but I felt terrifically relieved" (p. 143). Later, as I tried to determine whether Ruth was describing an illumination of her environment or a specifically localized light, I asked whether it was *a* light. She replied, "Yes. And it was the *same* light. . . . Its shape, it doesn't have—I could not describe to you any features that we would recognize as human, for example. Nothing like that. It was more a *feeling* than a visual thing" (p. 147). St. Teresa calls this a light "more clear than the sun" but adds that it "is a light not seen" (*Mysticism*, p. 285).

Andrew Greeley, in his study of mystical and other "paranormal" experiences, found that 14 percent of those who responded positively to his "mysticism question," reported a sense of being "bathed in light" as one of the elements. Perhaps more important is the fact that he found this sensation of light to be one of a cluster of elements that showed the strongest correlation with "positive affect balance," his measure of psychological health (pp. 77–78).

It must be stressed that light, however, like the sensation of presence, is by itself a motif without specific significance. I have occasionally, for example, found light — even "beings of light"— involved in the terrifying attacks of the classic nightmare (*The Terror*, pp. 49, 217, 218, 223, and 242). Perhaps the Christian scriptural reference to demons as "angels of light" is a reference to this potential for the inversion of the ordinary symbolism of lightness and darkness. In mystical experience it is the presence of light within the appropriate experiential context that is consistently associated with what Gen has called the "numinous." And Rudolf Otto, who coined the term *numinous* (to indicate the *felt* element of the *holy*), was clear in stating that "it has its wild and demonic forms and can sink to an almost grisly horror and shuddering" (*The Idea of the Holy*, p. 13).

Having discussed the five basic, describable elements of Gen's experience outlined above — (1) a very definite, *personal,* presence; (2) devoid of sensations; (3) wordlessly communicating and eliciting a flood of love; (4) accompanied by a non-physical light; and (5) persisting for about five days —, and having compared that experience to some similar and some dissimilar ones, what can be concluded with regard to the question of whether "mystical experience" comprises a single altered state of consciousness that may or may not appear "religious," depending on available language and explanatory frames? Gen's case clearly supports the hypothesis concerning mystical experience that I proposed above: There are several distinct and coherent forms of such experience; in at least some of these forms perceptions and information (James's "noetic quality") are as important as feelings in the emotional sense; the characteristics of these forms cannot be accounted for entirely on the basis of language or cultural input (although both are doubtless important); therefore, obviously, religious mystical experiences cannot be reduced to aberrant or localized forms of non-religious mystical experiences (p. 142). Her case also suggests that various kinds of these experiences have major experiential elements in common. There are a number of distinct kinds of mystical experience, recognizable on the basis of describable elements that are present in some but not in others. For example, the intellectual vision is characterized by a particular kind of sensation of presence; that sensation is often also found in the clearly different patterns of the NDE and the classic nightmare experience; and its absence is one of the definitive criteria of the "nature mystical" experience. We are dealing with elements and clusters of elements that are available to us for scientific investigation. That is not to say that we have understood or can fully understand what the mystic is attempting to describe concerning even the most straightforward elements; nor is it to say that the resulting systematization will be identical to those of the mystics or even useful to mystics. But it does mean that the empirical investigation of these experiences, in a way that seriously attempts to derive their phenomenology, is possible. Such investigation should not be avoided on the basis that they are "too subjective" or "ineffable." I would even go so far as to suggest that by such an experience-centered approach these religious experiences can be studied in a manner that provides mutual insight between the science of religion and the practice of religion, without reducing the one to the other.

Beyond this discussion of Gen's experience itself I want to add a consideration of what she has told us about her response to it and to compare this response to what the mystical literature says on the subject. St. Teresa, speaking of her own first experience of an intellectual vision, tells us that, in the tradition of career mystics, she immediately sought spiritual guidance from her confessor. However, he was not familiar with this phenomenon and asked her a great many questions about how she could have such knowledge without having seen or heard anything. Since she could not explain this any more than Gen can, the confessor and others from whom St. Teresa sought guidance "constantly cautioned her against this vision." But in spite of this she "was sure that it was no trick of her imagination . . . [and] she found it impossible to disbelieve in it" (p. 181). Because of the distress that she herself was caused by this inexperienced spiritual director, St. Teresa went on to stress the importance of finding a counselor who is knowledgeable and has deep personal experience of spirituality. Gen's situation was again very similar. Since she was not under analysis at the time of the vision she had no one to whom to turn immediately, certainly not anyone whom she could count on to be knowledgeable about such things. And yet she felt a need to know more about it; in a sense, to have it validated. Fortunately she had available a good library and the skill to use it. While she was still in the midst of the experience she made Evelyn Underhill and St. Teresa her "spiritual directors." The value of these two sources is shown by her statement that "it was of crucial importance to me to know that what had come so suddenly into my life was not something totally new and unknown, but that such an event had a name and had been experienced and understood centuries ago" (p. 44). This need is common to practically all who encounter mystical experiences of any kind, but most people today are not as fortunate in finding help so quickly. Nonetheless, books, however useful, are no substitute for the guidance of one with whom a two-way conversation is possible, and who is familiar with one's own language and frame of reference. In this, Gen was no more successful than St. Teresa seems to have been. "None of my various mentors understood it at all" (p. 44). I have already noted the reactions of her Jungian colleagues, ranging from considering the vision a "psychic curiosity" to Dr. Harding's advice that it was "to be mistrusted." And yet, like St. Teresa, Gen found that "the experience was so overwhelmingly good that I couldn't mistrust it. . . . It was the most important thing that had ever happened to me" (pp. 43, 45). She is also in agreement with the great mystical writers in finding that the goodness of the experience is in part demonstrated by its long-term effect. In our discussions I asked her if she felt the vision had made a difference in her subsequent life. She replied, "Yes, it has made a tremendous difference! Because I was aware of . . . a kind of spiritual support that I hadn't known before that. My ego was not so much involved; I could risk my ego. It doesn't matter." And again, in her memoir she has said that "it altered my life permanently, and that value of which I was permitted an awareness in those few days has for me transcended all others. . . . I have had ever since an intuitive awareness of being 'companioned.' That numinous figure is still there, I know, and it is the deficiency of my vision that prevents me from seeing it" (p. 48). As St. Teresa put it, "the benefits caused by this favor prove how great and valuable it is" (p. 183).

Another part of Gen's response to her vision is also widely shared. St. Teresa, speaking especially of that presence which she felt certain was Jesus Christ Himself, wrote: "Thus when the Lord chooses to withdraw his presence, the soul makes every possible effort to induce Him to return. This avails but little, for this grace comes at His will and not by our endeavors" (p. 183). When I asked Gen for details about the end of her vision, she said, "It ended on the Saturday of that week . . . and I felt badly. I wanted it to continue, but it just gradually faded." Afterward she made several attempts to bring the experience about again. From Evelyn Underhill's book she learned the concept of contemplative prayer and tried to develop this wordless technique. "I tried it systematically for a while, and was never able to get very far. Then, a good many years later, when we were first in Pittsburgh, in the fifties, I happened to have more free time so that I felt, 'Maybe this is when I'm meant to try this.' I would sit down every morning and see what I could do. But it didn't add up to much." Gen made one other attempt to both find guidance and perhaps learn to recapture her vision. She had been attending a Unitarian church and it occurred to her that the minister there might "have the makings of understanding," although as she now realizes "I'm sure I'd have done better in some other church, but I didn't have a connection anywhere else. . . . I still felt that I should be doing something about the experience and this man was quite a scholar. I thought that maybe he would know something about this. It really shook him, considerably! He asked me if I was menopausal at that point, so I decided I wasn't getting anywhere with him. I hadn't come to the menopause, and didn't for some time after that." When I asked her if that was his sole contribution, she continued, "Well, he was kind of embarrassed by the whole thing. He was really troubled, I thought. But to him it was clearly a disturbance." As I noted before, such disappointed efforts are among the major obstacles that our culture places in the way of open communication about this part of life.

Although Gen herself was unable either to recapture her experience or find personal guidance in connection with it, she did find an important opportunity to share it with another whom she was attempting to guide and help. She was counseling a student who was depressed and had attempted suicide. Just as Ruth decided that she should tell her sister of her near death experience in order to help her through the death of a friend, Gen decided to tell this student. "I had the feeling that if she could realize that there was another dimension to life, beyond the ones that she was taking into account, that it might help her. And I think it did." Whatever the role of this sharing in the process, Gen did succeed in helping the student to overcome her depression. I have found that people favored with such experiences often find that, despite the current barriers to open discussion, there is a feeling that others may at times be helped by such knowledge and that in these cases there is an obligation to give that help. But balance on this point is of great importance. Those who respond with what the mystical litera-

ture calls spiritual pride, and what Gen calls excessive ego involvement, often justify the decision
to publicize their experiences on the basis that
they are helping others. At the most mystically
aware times, the personal and social implications
of these experiences is a sensitive matter, requir-
ing the help of an excellent spiritual director. At
times such as the present, when both the experiences themselves and the concept of spiritual
direction are practically unknown, it is a wonder
that more people do not succumb to the inherent
dangers of the situation. Perhaps this is an indication of just how subtle and complex the noetic
quality of mystical experience can be.

Responding to this awareness, a man whom it
was my privilege to know found a strikingly modern solution. He was a physician who had a very
beautiful vision during the final year and a half of
his life, as he was dying from leukemia. In his
own case neither he nor those who cared for him
could doubt that the vision had had an enormously
positive effect on his ability to cope with the
rigors of his illness and its treatment. And, perhaps because he was himself a physician, he did
not seem very worried about how others would
react to his experience. Nonetheless, he was concerned that in telling people he might be "showing
off." At the same time he was sure that others
could be helped by knowing what he had seen (his
was not an intellectual vision). Although it cost
him a great deal of physical effort, he and I made
a videotape of his description of the vision and its
significance to him, and he asked me to use it to

help people. He then felt free to refer others to me and to the tape, comfortable in the knowledge that he had fulfilled an obligation and had done it in a way that spared him the risk of making himself the center of attention.

The mystics themselves, both career mystics and those like Gen who are taken completely by surprise when the numinous erupts in their lives, present us with a picture of extremely diverse kinds of experience, but a diversity within which there is order. They also show us that the response of the visionary is crucial in determining the actual value—personal and social—of each vision, and that the experiences are not ends but rather occasional accompaniments of spiritual development. Today our culture is impoverished in its knowledge both of visionary experience and of the appropriate response to it. For ideological reasons, enormous effort has been expended to reduce the varieties of mystical experience to an expedient number and nature. It is as though our culture itself has responded to this dimension of life with spiritual pride and egocentrism. To use Gen's image, we have attempted collectively to "set the mark of divinity" on our modern brow.

But there is currently a great resurgence of interest in and awareness of these matters in our society. This development has by no means sprung from a vacuum, but is rather a pivotal point in a very long historical process. Whether it will culminate in the development of new spiritual frameworks or the rejuvenation of old ones (Gen considers the former to be likely, while I favor the latter)

we are at a time when individual knowledge of
the transcendent has been officially suppressed to
the limit. Such suppression has always been fol-
lowed by spiritual revival and that is going on
now around the world. But never before has this
situation occurred in the context of instant communication, global mobility, and the constant ex-
posure of so many to the cultures of others. These
elements have both contributed to the process of
suppression and are now rendering the spiritual revival more chaotic. Whether this situation will
ultimately prove to be to our advantage or our dis-
advantage remains to be seen.

Whatever the outcome, our academic, medical,
and religious institutions all have a responsibility
to approach this subject more carefully and re-
spectfully than they have in recent years. This is
not to say that such academic subjects as psychology and anthropology should include spiritual
questions as if they were academic questions; nor
does it mean that medicine should consider part
of its primary mission to be spiritual, though
some in the (w)holistic health movement will dis-
agree with me here. It does mean that the academic
world and the medical world must recognize the
existence of spiritual questions as real, complex,
and important questions that must be distinguished from academic and medical questions.
This does not imply an academic or medical com-
mitment to a particular kind of answer to those
spiritual questions. It is like the need for medicine
to differentiate between quasi-mystical symptoms
of psychopathology and authentic mystical experi-

ence of the sort that Gen has clearly had, and this does not require that medicine even comment on the spiritual source or significance of that experience once pathology has been ruled out. At the same time there are questions that should be asked and empirically answered about these experiences which can be of spiritual as well as of academic and medical usefulness: How common are they? Who has them? What categories of experience and of interpretation can be objectively described? The list of such questions could be very long.

Our modern religious institutions face at least as great a challenge and bear at least as great a responsibility. The Judeo-Christian tradition, in all of its diversity, must recapture its ability to respond to personal, transcendent religion, and to a certain extent this effort has already begun. Since the eighteenth century Western religious institutions have produced increasingly secular and materialistic forms of religion. The persistence of mystical experience, without regard for institutional disapproval, among other factors, makes this trend appear wrongheaded. As Gen told her family, "God is not dead, but the mythology in which we did our thinking has lost its potency and fallen apart." This modern fall has not merely been permitted but has been actively encouraged by practically all modern institutions, including religious ones. Now it is time for these institutions to look for ways to participate in picking up the pieces. One way or another it appears that spiritual revival will continue in the modern world. Whether the ancient wisdom of Western religion and the modern wisdom of the academic and medical worlds will inform and benefit from that revival seems to depend on whether official Western institutions can find the humility to deal openly and gracefully with the people and the experiences that are involved.

Postscript

It is kind of my collaborator and of our editor to offer me the opportunity for a last word, but I find that almost everything has been said in the preceding pages. I confess I was startled at first, and a little amused, at the suggestion that my simple essay should be introduced to my fellow citizens by an anthropologist, as though I were a member of a newly discovered primitive tribe whose ways were too strange to be easily understood. It turns out that this is almost literally true and that the introduction and interpretation by David Hufford were the happiest of ideas. I am glad that he has found a place for me in the contemporary world, and more than glad to be introduced to those kindred others, whom I didn't know about, who have had experiences similar to mine. Although he and I come from such different backgrounds, we communicated easily from the first, except for a slight skirmish over the use of the word *union* in the description of mystical experience (see the footnote on p. 92). But since union in neither sense is part of my experience or my essay, the question is purely acadcmic here. For the rest, I feel myself fortunate for the chance (or was it chance?) that some of the readers at the University of Pittsburgh Press were acquainted with Dave's work and thus able to bring us together; and I especially thank him for his wise and understanding commentary.

GWF

Sources and
Selected Readings

This is not meant to be an exhaustive bibliography of mysticism. It gives full citations for the books and articles mentioned in our text and, for the interested reader, additional titles that represent each of the points of view we discuss. Brief annotations suggest the nature of the work listed where this can be helpful; page numbers in parentheses refer to the discussion in our text.

DJH

Augustine. *The Essential Augustine.* Selected and with commentary by Vernon J. Bourke. New York: The New American Library, 1964. The quote is from *Literal Commentary on Genesis,* trans. J. H. Taylor, S. J., p. 95. (P. 169)

Bourke, Linda B., and Kurt W. Back. "Language, Society, and Subjective Experience." *Sociometry* 34 (1971):1–21. (Pp. 126–27)

Bradburn, Norman M. *The Structure of Psychological Well-Being.* Chicago: Aldine Press, 1969. (P. 95)

Capps, Walter Holden, and Wendy M. Wright, eds. *Silent Fire: An Invitation to Western Mysticism.* New York: Harper & Row, 1978. The main writings of the major figures of Western mysticism. Each selection is accompanied by a brief introductory essay. Concludes with eight pages of good suggestions for further reading.

Sources and Selected Readings

Comfort, Alex. *I and That: Notes on the Biology of Religion.* New York: Crown Publishers, 1979. (P. 114)

———. "On Going to the Forest: Geriatrics and Pastoral Thanatology." *Journal of Operational Psychiatry* 2 (1980): 38–40. (Pp. 112, 114–15, 130)

The Committee on Psychiatry and Religion of the Group for the Advancement of Psychiatry. *Mysticism: Spiritual Quest or Pyschic Disorder?* Vol. 9, Publication 97. New York: The Group for the Advancement of Psychiatry, November 1976. (Pp. 99–100)

———. *The Psychic Function of Religion in Mental Illness and Health.* Vol. 6, Report 67. New York: The Group for the Advancement of Psychiatry, January 1968. (P. 104)

Edinger, Edward F. *Ego and Archetype.* New York: G. P. Putnam's Sons, 1972. (P. 41)

Eidelberg, Ludwig, ed. *The Encyclopedia of Psychoanalysis.* New York: The Free Press, 1968. (P. 115)

Eissler, Kurt. "Creativity and Adolescence: The Effect of Trauma in Freud's Adolescence." In *Psychoanalytic Study of the Child,* vol. 33. New Haven: Yale University Press, 1978. (P. 63–64)

Ellwood, Robert S., Jr. *Mysticism and Religion.* Englewood Cliffs, N.J.: Prentice-Hall, 1980. (P. 138)

Erikson, Erik H. *Childhood and Society.* New York: Norton, 1964.

———. "Reflections on Dr. Borg's Life Cycle." In *Adulthood,* ed. Erik H. Erikson. New York: W. W. Norton, 1978. (Pp. 79–80)

Favazza, Armando, R., and Ahmed Faheem, with commentary by Alex Comfort, Joan Koss, E. Mansell Pattison, E. Wittkower, and G. MacLean. "The Heavenly Vision of a Poor Woman." *Journal of Operational Psychiatry* 10 (1979): 93–126.

> This case report, taken together with the excellent and very diverse set of comments that follows it, illustrates both the existence of cases of psychopathology in which reports of visionary experiences and religious ideation figure prominently and the sociocultural and psychiatric difficulties involved in their proper diagnosis and treatment. This is very useful because these cases represent the kind of pathological category to which some writers have attempted to reduce all mystical experience.

Freud, Sigmund. *Civilization and Its Discontents.* Trans. Joan Riviere. Rev. and ed. James Strachey. The International Psychoanalytic Library, No. 17. London: The Hogarth Press, 1972. Originally published in English in 1930 by Hogarth Press. (P. 115)

Gallup, George, Jr., with William Proctor. *Adventures in Immortality: A Look Beyond the Threshold of Death.* New York: McGraw-Hill, 1982.

The writing of this book was apparently triggered by recent interest in near death experiences, although it places the NDE in a larger context than most other works on the subject, including other kinds of religious experience and the beliefs of the U.S. population. Gallup's survey research reported here is very useful and interesting. The text of the book is popular in style and not always easy to connect with the extensive numerical data given in the appendix.

Goldstein, Diane E. "The Language of Religious Experience and Its Implications for Fieldwork." *Western Folklore* 40 (1983): 105–13.

The author discusses the difficulties of understanding the metaphors and analogies that characterize the language of religious experience. For her examples she uses personal experience narratives from members of the congregation of an "ecumenical occult/metaphysical church in Philadelphia" (p. 107), and uses C. S. Lewis's "Transposition" for part of her analysis of this language.

Goleman, Daniel, and Richard J. Davidson, eds. *Consciousness: Brain, States of Awareness, and Mysticism.* New York: Harper & Row, 1979.

A collection of introductory readings reprinted from various sources divided into the following parts: "The Brain and Consciousness," "Ordinary States of Consciousness," "Altered States of Consciousness," and "The Politics of Consciousness." Comments concerning mysticism are here intermixed with other states of consciousness including drug intoxication and psychotic states. Although the collection tends to be reductionistic it does include an interesting rejoiner to GAP's *Mysticism: Spiritual Quest or Psychic Disorder?* written by Arthur Deikman and reprinted from the *Journal of Nervous and Mental Disease* (pp. 191–94).

Greeley, Andrew M. *Ecstasy: A Way of Knowing.* Englewood Cliffs, N.J.: Prentice-Hall, 1974.

This is a more general discussion, without all the statistical analysis, of the study that Greeley reported in his *The Sociology of the Paranormal: A Reconnaissance.*

———. *The Sociology of the Paranormal: A Reconnaissance.* Sage Research Papers in the Social Sciences, vol. 3, series 90–023 (Studies in Religion and Ethnicity). Beverly Hills: Sage Publications, 1975. (Pp. 92–98, 122, 130, 172)

Greenacre, Phyllis. "The Family Romance of the Artist." In *Psychoanalytic Study of the Child,* vol. 13. New Haven: Yale University Press, 1958. (Pp. 60–61)

Grof, Stanislav, and Christina Grof. *Beyond Death: The Gates of Consciousness.* London: Thames and Hudson, 1980.
  This book begins with a discussion of ancient and modern views on altered states of consciousness, near death experiences, beliefs about an afterlife, and ritual encounters with death. The remainder of the book examines themes from many cultures and times relating to death and afterlife. The latter portion is heavily illustrated and is very useful for the comparison of motifs and patterns from different traditions.

Grof, Stanislav, and J. Halifax. *The Human Encounter with Death.* New York: Dutton, 1977.
  A description of research on the administration of LSD to cancer patients as a part of psychotherapy. The authors discuss the similarities between the death-and-rebirth experiences of their patients and other kinds of mystical experiences and explain the patterns within a Jungian framework.

Happold, F. C. *Mysticism: A Study and an Anthology.* Hammondsworth, Middlesex, England: Penguin Books, 1963.
  The first 122 pages of this book present an excellent introduction to the various forms and interpretations of mysticism. The final 278 pages present readings from many different mystical traditions, including Christian, Hindu, and Sufi, although Christian readings predominate. Each section in the anthology is preceded by very useful headnotes.

Heaney, John J. "Recent Studies of Near-Death Experiences." *Journal of Religion and Health* 22 (1983): 116–30.
  Summarizes recent work about NDEs and then presents a Jungian interpretation of them.

Hood, Ralph W., Jr. "Mystical Experience as Related to Present and Anticipated Future Church Participation." *Psychological Reports* 39 (1976): 1127–36. (P. 150)

Hood, Ralph W., Jr., and Ronald J. Morris. "Toward a Theory of Death Transcendence." *Journal for the Scientific Study of Religion* 22 (1983): 353–65.
  "A preliminary (cognitive) theory of death transcendence is proposed that neither assumes that persons are pervasively motivated to 'deny death' nor that immortality is conceptually or empirically impossible. . . . In addition, the special linkage between cognitive modes of death transcendence and mysticism is discussed" (p. 353). This article includes a report of survey research concerning the consequences of a variety of orientations toward death, including mystical orientations, in terms of such factors as fear of death.

190

Hoyt, Michael F. "Clinical Notes Regarding the Experience of 'Presences' in Mourning." *Omega* 11 (1980): 105–11. (P. 122)

Hufford, David J. "Ambiguity and the Rhetoric of Belief." *Keystone Folklore Quarterly* 21 (1976): 11–24.

A discussion of ambiguity in the language of mystical experience both as an intentional defense used by visionaries to avoid excessive disclosure and as a methodological problem for scholars of mystical experience.

———. *The Terror That Comes in the Night: An Experience-Centered Study of Supernatural Assault Traditions.* Philadelphia: University of Pennsylvania Press, 1982. (Pp. 119–23, 172)

———. "Traditions of Disbelief." *New York Folklore Quarterly* 8, no. 3–4 (Winter 1982): 47–56.

———. "The Supernatural and the Sociology of Knowledge: Explaining Academic Belief." *New York Folklore Quarterly* 9, no. 1–2 (Winter 1983): 21–30.

These two articles discuss and analyze systematic biases in the academic study of supernatural belief, with particular reference to scientistic ideology.

Huxley, Aldous. *The Doors of Perception.* London: Chatto and Windus, 1954. (Pp. 110, 124–25)

James, William. *The Varieties of Religious Experience: A Study in Human Nature.* New York: Longmans, Green, 1902. Reprint. New York: Modern Library, Random House, n.d. (Pp. 94, 124, 163)

Jung, C. G. *Collected Works.* Ed. G. Adler et al. 20 vols. Bollingen Series. Princeton: Princeton University Press, 1954–79).

Kelsey, Morton. *Encounter with God: A Theology of Christian Experience.* Minneapolis: Bethany Fellowship, 1972.

This book contains a very useful overview of developments within Christianity concerning the reality of the supernatural and "sets forth [the] thesis that there is a spiritual reality that impinges on man's consciousness, and the consequences of an appreciation of this reality for the life of the church and the individual Christian today" (Rev. John A. Sanford, from the book's cover). Kelsey incorporates a great deal of Jungian psychology in his presentation.

Kristo, Jure. "The Interpretation of Mystical Experience: What Do Mystics Intend When They Talk About Their Experiences?" *The Journal of Religion* 61 (1981): 21–38.

The author treats mystical experiences as culturally shaped psychological events. He concludes that despite their ontological assertions, "mystics want primarily to engage in *theological* discussions. Their experience is only an occasion for this discussion. Often this experience is also the 'proof' of already existing theological and scriptural positions" (p. 38). Kristo's arguments are, in large part, directly contrary to those that I have presented in this book, and his paper is a good illustration of the conventional point of view.

Kroll, Jerome, and Bernard Bachrach. "Visions and Psychopathology in the Middle Ages." *The Journal of Nervous and Mental Disease* 170 (1982): 41–49.

"Descriptions of visionary experiences from written medieval sources are examined from a cross-cultural perspective" (p. 41). The medieval cultural support for visionary experiences as real and not pathological is documented, and the authors also report that few of the recorded medieval visions appear related to psychopathology even by today's standards.

La Barre, Weston. "Anthopological Perspectives on Hallucination and Hallucinogens." In *Hallucinations: Behavior, Experience, and Theory*, ed. R. K. Siegel and L. J. West, pp. 9–52. New York: John Wiley & Sons, 1975.

This is a good example of the anthropological approach to the reduction of visionary states to hallucinations. La Barre, a major figure in the psychiatric anthropology of religion, makes his philosophy clear in the following quote: "Let everyone be epistemologically tidy about the location of these various realities: the supernatural is wholly housed in the subconscious" (p. 18).

Levinson, D. J., et al. *The Seasons of a Man's Life.* New York: Ballantine Books, 1979. (Pp. 50, 78–79)

Lewis, C. S. "Transposition." In *The Weight of Glory and Other Addresses*, ed. Walter Hooper, pp. 54–73. New York: MacMillan, 1975. Originally published in 1949.

This essay by one of the most popular Christian authors of this century addresses the problem of the manner in which humans appear to perceive invisible spiritual realities. Lewis's analogies and discussion are very helpful with regard to all kinds of religious visions.

MacDonald, W. Scott, and Chester W. Oden, Jr. "*Amakua:* Behavioral Direction Visions in Hawaiians." *Journal of Abnormal Psychology* 86 (1977): 189–94. (P. 122)

Maslow, Abraham H. *Religions, Values and Peak-Experiences.* New York: Penguin Books, 1976. (Pp. 113–14)

Matchett, William Foster. "Repeated Hallucinatory Experiences as a Part of the Mourning Process Among Hopi Women." *Psychiatry* 35 (1972): 185–94. (P. 122)

Sources and Selected Readings

Merton, Thomas. *The Ascent to Truth.* New York: Harcourt, Brace, 1951. (P. 103)

An exposition of the teachings of the sixteenth-century Carmelite mystic, St. John of the Cross, by the most popular mystical writer of recent times. Merton was himself a Cistercian (Trappist) priest.

Moody, Raymond A., Jr. *Life After Life.* Atlanta: Mockingbird Books, 1975. (Pp. 131–33, 137, 139–42)

Noyes, Russell, Jr. "The Human Experience of Death; or, What Can We Learn from Near-Death Experiences?" *Omega* 13 (1982–83): 251–59.

"The changes in attitudes, personality, and beliefs that sometimes follow these experiences reflect rebirth and reveal a fundamental human strategy for coping with the threat of death. . . . These experiences appear to have much to teach us about the human encounter with death and to have great therapeutic potential, providing we can learn how to use them" (p. 251). This article summarizes the current thinking of the most systematic researcher of NDEs and the one who has studied them longest (since before Raymond Moody's *Life After Life* brought the subject to widespread attention and before the term "near death experience" had been coined).

Otto, Rudolf. *The Idea of the Holy.* Trans. John W. Harvey. London: Oxford University Press, 1953. (P. 172)

Pahnke, Walter N., and William A. Richards. "Implications of LSD and Experimental Mysticism." *Journal of Religion and Health* 5 (1966): 175–208.

This is one of the major early articles on this subject. It includes an analysis of the categories of mystical experience derived from a review of the historical literature of mysticism and a description of a controlled and double-blind experiment using psilocybin to facilitate mystical experience in a religious setting.

Persinger, Michael A. "Religious and Mystical Experiences as Artifacts of Temporal Lobe Function: A General Hypothesis." *Perceptual and Motor Skills* 57 (1983): 1255–62.

"Mystical and religious experiences are hypothesized to be evoked by transient, electrical microseizures within deep structures of the temporal lobe" (p. 1255). The author treats these events as normal but existing on a continuum with pathological seizures. He examines similarities between electrically caused changes of consciousness and the categories of religious and mystical experiences and uses his hypothesized physical mechanism to explain cross-cultural patterns in these experiences. This hypothesis has the virtue of being empirically testable, but in its present form it already makes some predictions that experiences like Gen Foster's do not fulfill.

Price, George. "Science and the Supernatural." *Science* 122 (1955): 359–67. (Pp. 160–61)

Rees, W. Dewi. "The Hallucinations of Widowhood." *British Medical Journal* (2 Oct. 1971): 37–41. (P. 122)

Richards, William A. "Mystical and Archetypal Experiences of Terminal Patients in DPT-Assisted Psychotherapy." *Journal of Religion and Health* 17 (1978): 117–26.

Written by Walter Pahnke's co-author of "Implications of LSD and Experimental Mysticism" (1966), this paper documents positive therapeutic gains using dipropyltryptamine. The author uses a Jungian framework.

Ring, Kenneth. *Life at Death: A Scientific Investigation of the Near-Death Experience.* New York: Coward, McCann & Geoghegan, 1980. (Pp. 142, 150, 171)

Rousseau, Jean-Jacques. *Emile, or On Education.* Trans. Allan Bloom. New York: Basic Books, 1979. (Pp. 65–66)

Sabom, Michael B. *Recollections of Death: A Medical Investigation.* New York: Harper & Row, 1982. (P. 142)

Sagan, Carl. "The Amniotic Universe." In *Broca's Brain: Reflections on the Romance of Science.* New York: Random House, 1974. Pp. 301–14.

A discussion of the near death experience using Stanislav Grof's work with LSD and experimental mysticism to propose that memories of the experience of birth are the source of cross-cultural patterns found in NDEs. Sagan then uses this conclusion to sketch a "rationalistic explanation of religious belief" (p. 310). Although written as a popular essay this does illustrate another of the conventional academic perspectives that argue for the reduction of visionary and mystical experiences to a form of naive misunderstanding of natural events.

Saler, Benson. "Supernatural as a Western Category." *Ethos* 5 (Spring 1977): 31–53. (P. 88)

Siegel, Ronald K. "The Psychology of Life After Death." *American Psychologist* 35 (1980): 911–31.

This article discusses recent near-death-experience research and religious beliefs about an afterlife and concludes that "the similarity of afterlife visions to drug-induced hallucinations invites a rational framework for their experimental analysis. . . . [They] can be interpreted as evidence that people survive death, but . . .

may be more easily understood as a dissociative hallucinatory activity of the brain" (p. 911). Siegel's review of the literature is useful. This article is not closely argued, being rather popular in tone, but it illustrates well the conventional reductive approach to visions as wish-fulfilling hallucinations.

Slavson, S. R. *An Introduction to Group Therapy.* New York: Commonwealth Fund, 1943. (P. 16)

Smythies, J. R. "A Logical and Cultural Analysis of Hallucinatory Sense-Experience." *Journal of Mental Science* (now called the *British Journal of Psychiatry*) 102 (1956): 336–42.

The author analyzes "the attitudes of people toward their own hallucinations and the attitudes of other people toward people who have hallucinations in our own and other cultures" and presents "a phenomenological classification of hallucinations" (p. 336). Both religious visions and the typical hallucinations of psychotic states are considered, and the author cautiously raises questions about criteria for deciding whether an experience is "real." He also briefly contrasts the Freudian and Jungian perspectives on hallucinations.

Stettner, John W. "What to Do with Visions." *Journal of Religion and Health* 13 (1974): 229–38.

The author asks "what are we to do with these phenomena (visions) that are described in the Bible, how are we to understand them, and whether there are any such things going on today?" (p. 229). He concludes that visions do still occur and suggests four points for the modern response to them: "take them for real," "pay attention to them," "try to understand them," and "use them by integrating them into life" (p. 238). He quotes and discusses the visionary experiences of Anton Boisen and Carl Jung. The article is written from a pastoral counseling perspective.

Stevenson, Ian. "Do We Need a New Word to Supplement 'Hallucination'?" *American Journal of Psychiatry* 140 (1983): 1609–11.

Stevenson suggests the word *idiophany* as a neutral term for "unshared sensory experiences" because of the pathological implications of "hallucination."

Surin, Jean-Joseph. *Histoire littéraire du sentiment religieux en France.* Quoted in Robert Plank, "On Seeing the Salamander." In *Psychoanalytic Study of the Child,* vol. 12, p. 387. New York: International Universities Press, 1957. (P. 69)

Teresa, Saint (of Avila). *The Interior Castle, or The Mansions. Translated from the Spanish by a Benedictine Monk of Stanbrook Abbey.* Introduction and notes by Father Benedict Zimmerman, O.C.D. Union City, N.J.: John J. Crawley, 1980. Originally published in 1577. This translation was first published in 1912. (Pp. 165–69, 176–77)

Thompson, C. "*Anwesenheit:* Psychopathology and Clinical Associations." *British Journal of Psychiatry* 141 (1982): 628–30. (Pp. 161–65)

Underhill, Evelyn. *Mysticism: A Study in the Nature and Development of Man's Spiritual Consciousness.* New York: E. P. Dutton, 1961. Originally published in 1911. (Pp. 46–48, 92, 99, 165, 168, 175, 177)

Vaisrub, Samuel. "Afterthoughts on Afterlife." *Archives of Internal Medicine* 137 (1977): 150. (P. 139)

Weston, Jessie. *From Ritual to Romance.* New York: Doubleday, 1957.

Zaehner, R. C. *Mysticism: Sacred and Profane. An Inquiry Into Some Varieties of Praeternatural Experience.* London: Oxford University Press, 1961. Originally published in 1957 by Clarendon Press. (Pp. 110–11)

    Zaehner uses a great variety of mystical literature, both Eastern and Western, to argue for the existence of fundamental differences between monistic mysticism and theistic mysticism. Throughout the book he presents a set of specific counterarguments to the position taken by Aldous Huxley in *The Doors of Perception* (1954).

Index

Index

Buddhism, 115
Buddhist mysticism, 110
Bulletin of the Analytical Psychology Club, 27–30, 34, 41

Campbell, Joseph, 52
Cannabis, 124
Career mystics, 124, 166
Catherine, St. (of Siena), 101
Cathexis, 64
Centering process, 78
Charismatic gifts, 98
Charismatics, 129
Childhood, 54–57, 59–63
Christ. *See* Jesus Christ
Christianity, 69, 71, 115
Church, 141; Catholic, 158, 159. *See also* Mysticism
Comfort, Alex, 112, 114–16, 118, 130, 156, 160
Communication, nonverbal, 132, 136, 137
Complex, central, 46
Conscience, 23, 81
Contact with the dead, 93, 122. *See also* Ghosts
Contemplation, infused, 102–03
Conversion experience, 46, 69
Counseling. *See* Guidance
Creativity, 7, 21, 34, 49, 61, 63, 64, 78
Cultural shaping, 105–06, 116–52 passim, 147, 149, 153, 159, 173
Cultural source hypothesis, 119–20, 131
Cupid, 75

Death, 77, 79, 81, 178; and development, 54; attitudes toward, 111–12, 131, 133; fear of, 111–12, 139; irrelevance of, 111–12, 115; in Genevieve Foster's life, 35. *See also* Afterlife; Bereavement; Dream(s) of resisting death; Mourning; Near death experience
Defense mechanisms, 101, 118
Delusion, 7, 108
Demerol, 146
Demons, 88
Denial. *See* Reality, denial of
Depression, 178

Desdemona, 66
Desire, 39
Development, human. *See* Adolescence; Biological change and development; Childhood; Individuation process; Mid-life; Oedipal stage; Old age
Developmental crises, 5
Devil, 20, 21, 40
Dionysus, cult of, 71–77
Dream(s), 15, 30, 31, 51, 79, 119; Genevieve Foster's, analyzed by Jung, 20–21; of levitation, 42; of resisting death, 82, 83; of "safari," 80–82; of wings, 42
Drugs. *See* Demerol; Hallucinogens; Hashish; Intoxication; LSD; Levodopa; Mescalin; Nitrous oxide

Ecstasy, 58, 60, 95, 111, 138, 142
Edinger, Edward F., 24–25, 41
Education Group of the Analytical Psychology Club, 11–22, 25, 34
Ego, 8, 33, 41, 43, 47–48, 51, 68, 77, 78, 167, 176, 179, 180. *See also* Pride, spiritual
Elation, 70
Eliot, T. S., 40
Ellen, 25, 27
Ellwood, Robert S., Jr., 138
Emotions. *See* Awe; Elation; Humor; Joy; Love; Mourning; Peace; Rapture
Epilepsy: and mystical experience, 99, 164; temporal lobe, 162. *See also* Seizure(s)
Episcopal church, 159
Erikson, Erik H., 5, 50, 53, 54, 58, 63, 79
Eriny(e)s, 75–76
Estelle, 16
Ethnocentrism, 113–14, 129, 138, 156
Evil, 119, 121

Fantasies, archetypal, 5
Fantasy, 2, 15, 51, 52, 55–58, 63–65, 67, 79, 100, 157; religious, 104. *See also* Imagination; Play
Faun, 73

Index

Index

Index

Nitrous oxide, 124, 130
Noetic quality, 94, 142, 173, 179
Nordfeldt, Margaret, 33–34, 44
Numinous, 42, 43, 48, 90, 106, 172, 176, 180
Nymph, 74

Oceanic experience or feeling, 61, 114–15, 130, 160
Oedipal stage, 53, 56, 59
Old age, 59, 70, 78–83, 114–15
Ophelia, 66
Other, the, 5, 42, 47, 54, 58
Otto, Rudolf, 172
Out of body experience, 97, 132–33, 135–37, 140. *See also* Near death experience

Pain, 134–35, 143, 146
Panisks, 72
Paralysis. *See* Sleep paralysis
Parents, 53, 58, 77, 79, 100
Parthenogenesis, 65
Paul, St., 99, 141
Paulsen, Alma, 12, 25
Peace, 70, 133, 141
Peak experience(s), 113–14, 138
Penitential practices, 164
Perception, false, 89. *See also* Hallucination(s)
Perceptual changes, 124
Perennial Philosophy, 110–17, 125, 130–31, 139, 159
Phallus: awe of, and mystical experience, 101; sacred, 71, 74, 76; worship, 61–62, 76
Phenomenology, 131, 174
Play, 51, 55–57, 58, 62–63
Polysemia, 128
Pompeii, 71
Postivism, logical, 88
Possession, 72–73
Prayer, 69, 130*n*, 164; contemplative, 177
Presence(s), 43, 48, 68, 121–22, 136–37, 160–70, 173, 176–77. *See also* *Anwesenheit*; Vision, intellectual
Pressure, 121
Preternatural, definition of, 88
Price, George, 160–61

Pride, 33; spiritual, 166–67, 179–80. *See also* Ego
Priestess, Dionysian, 72, 74
Projection, 6, 23, 26, 29, 34, 41–42, 46–47, 54, 77
Protestantism, 33, 42, 159
Psychoanalysis. *See* Freudian theory; Group for the Advancement of Psychiatry; Jungian analysis
Psychological set, 125, 131. *See also* Belief, prior; Cultural shaping
Psychopompos, 82
Psychosis, 29, 42–43, 100–01, 164–65; and presence(s), 162; and hallucinations, 103–04
Puberty, 62–63
Purgation, mystical, 40

Quakers (Society of Friends), 46, 159

Ramakrishna, 114
Rapture, 95
Rationalism, 43, 48, 70. *See also* Positivism, logical; Reductionism; Secular explanations
Reality: denial of, 100, 114–15; impression of, 2, 49, 121–22, 158, 162, 163, 168, 175; testing, 100, 104, 149
Rebirth, and mystical experience, 100
Reductionism, and mystical experience, 61, 98–109, 109–16, 142. *See also* Positivism, logical; Rationalism; Secular explanations
Reid, Forrest, 110
Relativism, cultural, 88
Religion, 47, 157–59, 160–61, 174; and mental health, 104–05; and mystical experience, 150–51; and mysticism, 89, 102, 109–16; biological basis of, 114–15; Eastern, 110, 114–15; Roman, classical, 71–76; secular, 117, 182; Western, 106, 151, 181–83
Religious feeling, 61, 68, 101
Religious institutions, 107, 109
Revival meetings, 69
Ring, Kenneth, 171
Ritual, 159
Rorschach: ink-blots, 114; Test, 11

Index

Rousseau, Jean-Jacques, 65–66
Ruth, 134–38, 143–52, 170–71, 178

Sallie, 16, 17, 18, 19, 21–22, 24, 25–26
Sanskrit, 15
Scapegoat, 19, 22, 26
Schizophrenia. See Mystical experience and schizophrenia
Scripture, 172
Secular explanations, 61, 88, 117–20, 131, 149–50, 154–55, 161
Seizure(s) and mystical experience, 100
Self, the, 42, 58, 77
Seventh Day Adventists, 150
Sexual feelings, 62
Shadow side, 6
Shakespeare, William, 70
Shamanism, 130
Silenus, 72, 73
Sleep disturbances, 162–64
Sleep paralysis, 120–22
Social control, 107–09, 118
Sonnets, Genevieve Foster's, 31–32, 34–36, 37–39, 39–41
Soul, 20, 82, 155, 166, 167
Spirit(s), 132, 140, 157, 167–68. See also Angels; Demons; Devil; Ghosts; God; Supernatural persons
Spirituality, 119, 180–83
Suffering, mystery of, 91
Suffragists, 64
Suicide, 137, 178
Supernal light. See Light
Supernatural, 74, 87–90, 118, 131, 149, 156; assault traditions of, 119–22, 163–64; belief in, 96, 105–06, 112–16, 118–23, 129, 149, 150, 160–61; definition of, 88–89; persons, 76, 118, 131–52, 160–61
Surin, Jean-Joseph, S.J., 69
Survival of death, 82, 95–96, 111–12, 115, 139–42. See also Near death experience; Spirit(s)
Symbol(ism), 15, 33, 35, 52, 155, 157, 172. See also Metaphor; Sonnets

Talisman, 31
Teresa, St. (of Avila), 48, 99, 103, 114, 165–69, 174–77

Theism, 112
Thinking function, 49
Thompson, C., 161–65
Time sense, 124, 135–36
Traherne, Thomas, 59–60
Trance, 99–100
Transcendence, 111, 126–27
Transference, 6, 9, 30
Types, psychological, 26–27

Unconscious, the, 3–6, 9, 10, 13, 17, 31, 33, 35, 49, 51, 52, 63, 64, 68, 83; collective, 63, 153–57. See also Archetype(s)
Underhill, Evelyn, 44, 46–48, 92, 99, 124, 130, 165, 168, 175, 177
Unicorn, 40–41
Union. See Mystical union; Unitive Life
Unitarian church, 177–78
Unitive Life, 92
Utopias, 64–65

Vaisrub, Samuel, 139
Validation, consensual, 103–06
Value: central, 29, 35, 39, 47, 77; ultimate, 71
Vampirism, 119
Vaughan, Henry, 60
Villa of Mysteries, 71
Vision(s), 50–51, 79–80, 122, 157; definition of, 87–88; Genevieve Foster's, 42–44; intellectual, 2, 41, 48, 158, 160–70, 174–75; St. Catherine's, 101. See also Anwesenheit; Presence(s)

Wholistic health movement, 181
Waste Land, The, 40
Whitmont, Dr., 24
Wickes, Frances, 15, 44
Wings. See Dream(s), of wings
Wish fulfillment, 139
Witchcraft, 119
Wordsworth, William, 59–60

Xenoglossy, 98

Yeats, William Butler, 81, 82